Akron's
Infamous
Escort Case

JANE BOND

THE
History
PRESS

Published by The History Press
Charleston, SC
www.historypress.com

First published 2023

Manufactured in the United States

ISBN 9781467153454

Library of Congress Control Number: 2022918029

Notice: The information in this book is true and complete to the best of our knowledge. It is offered without guarantee on the part of the author or The History Press. The author and The History Press disclaim all liability in connection with the use of this book.

To Melissa Hunt Sublett and all the women who lost their lives to addiction.

CONTENTS

CONTENTS

PREFACE

T his is a true story that took place in Akron, Ohio, more than twenty
years ago. It is a story of lust, betrayal, ambition and murder. You
can decide what you believe and who you think was responsible for
what happened. The story is told from my perspective. I presided over the
cases that collectively became the "Escort Case." I am a retired Common
Pleas judge in Summit County, Ohio. In telling the story, I have been as
factually accurate as possible, relying on word-for-word transcripts, tape
recordings, newspaper articles, my personal notes and my own memory. You
can proceed step by step with me as the facts are discovered.

The American criminal justice system is a complex series of statutes
and rules that are intended to balance opposing interests and produce a
just result. In this case, that balance was thrown off. Understanding what
happened and why can help us see where the system needs to be changed
and where we need to be vigilant. To aid in understanding what happened,
I offer an introduction to the key participants. Keeping everyone and their
roles straight isn't easy. You will have to decide what you believe as the
evidence is presented. Unlike fiction, reality isn't a contrived narrative,
with everything neatly resolved in the last chapter. Were there heroes and
villains? Who bears responsibility for the course the cases took? Was justice
done in the end?

ACKNOWLEDGEMENTS

I owe a huge debt of gratitude to Judge Elinore Marsh Stormer for her editing, suggestions, wisdom and encouragement throughout the project. William Ketler went back into painful memories to tell the story of Melissa Sublett with accuracy and compassion. My deep appreciation for his courage and honesty. Wendy Bartlett, friend and librarian, provided her professional resources, advice and editing skills. Thanks and thanks again. Eric Czetli was a patient, helpful reader from the very beginning. Judy Montgomery Casey and W. Paul Jeffrey were also eager, perceptive readers. Several people shared their memories and perspectives. Thanks to Tom Adgate, Don Malarcik, Judge Judy Nicely, Judge Carol Deszo, Terri Sims, Scott Reilly, Tom Ciccolini and Major Larry Limbert. I am very grateful to them all. I relied on the work of several talented journalists in constructing the narrative and giving the reader a sense of the contemporaneous view of events and personalities. Thanks to Bob Dyer, Stuart Warner, Dennis McEaneney, Margaret Newkirk and Eric Mansfield, as well as photojournalists Phil Long and Ed Suba Jr. Thanks also to Chip Bok, whose editorial cartoons in the *Akron Beacon Journal* were brilliant. Photographer extraordinaire Bruce Ford and Natalie Steen also have my thanks.

INTRODUCTION

These are the key participants in what became known as the "Escort Case."

Jack Porter was an Akron policeman who started as an entry-level patrolman and over twenty-eight years worked up to the rank of lieutenant. He was a polarizing figure on the force. A charismatic, devil-may-care man, Porter enjoyed life on his own terms. Some of his fellow officers loved him, but some thought that his personality and lifestyle were unsuitable for a law enforcement officer. He was known to stop a weaving car, and instead of arresting the driver, Jack put him in the patrol car, drove him home, told him to sober up and get help with his drinking. Few officers took that approach. Porter was lean and attractive and had an active social life, drinking in the bars in the Portage Lakes area. Completing the picture, Porter was lead singer in the rock band Sergeant Jack's Nightwatch. He admired Mick Jagger, dressing and singing like him. The band played in those same bars at the Portage Lakes where Porter frequently drank. The band also played at civic events, political fundraisers for elected officials and at private parties. They were good musicians. Jack was a versatile singer with a repertoire that reached from Sinatra standards to raunchy rock. Porter might have gone into music as a career, but he enjoyed working as a police officer.

Donald Fulkerson was an Akron police officer serving in the Vice Squad and almost the flip side of Jack Porter. A married man with four children, Fulkerson was active in his Catholic parish, respected in his community and well-liked by most of the police officers. He loved his work and had dreamed of being a police officer since childhood. Don was quiet, without Porter's flash, but sometimes those opposites do attract. Fulkerson became Jack's wing man, his backup. With Porter, Fulkerson experienced a side of life otherwise unknown to him.

Tom Adgate was a well-known Akron lawyer. He was slim, medium height with sandy red hair and sharp facial features. He reminded me of a fox. Tom's life was not without pain and struggle. He had serious emotional issues and at one time had self-medicated with alcohol. When he slid out of the bottle and into AA, he created a good life. He climbed out of the black hole of addiction and then decided to help every person he possibly could. He wasn't just a sponsor in AA; he was on call twenty-four-hours a day for anyone who needed him. He met his wife at an AA meeting. He was compassionate and intelligent and had a marvelous sense of humor that he expressed in his wit. Tom saw the failings in human nature, and he didn't judge—he empathized and offered help.

Michael Callahan was the county prosecutor. A large, beefy, red-haired, bearded Irishman, he was aggressive, fond of drinking and proud of his Irish heritage. Callahan worked as a bouncer during law school. His nickname was "Turk," and he displayed it on a vanity license plate on his car, a dark-blue Cadillac. Many of his friends were lawyers, and he socialized with them frequently. Callahan was confident. His career was going well. Callahan was politically ambitious. He sought and received an appointment to the Akron Municipal Court. After two years as a municipal judge, he sought another appointment as a Summit County Common Pleas judge. He was serving as a Common Pleas judge when an opening occurred in the Summit County Prosecutor's Office, and he wanted the job. He received another appointment and left the judiciary. He saw the prosecutor's job as a more powerful position than a judgeship. In many respects, he was right.

Judith Bandy was known as Judie. She was an experienced assistant Summit County prosecutor. She was smart, disciplined, intense and devoted to law enforcement. She firmly believed that she was working on the side of the angels, and she did so with complete commitment. She thrived on complex cases with hundreds of documents, multiple defendants, lengthy indictments and the opportunity to go head to head with defense lawyers. Judie spent hours and hours in her office organizing evidence, reviewing reports and interviewing witnesses. Although married, she had no children, and her dedication to her job kept her in the office evenings and weekends. Thin to the point of being gaunt, she seemed to live on coffee and cigarettes. She wore severely tailored suits but no jewelry or makeup—she was all business.

Larry Smith was an experienced criminal defense lawyer who had some rough days in his past. Of average height and build, he would never turn heads in a crowd, but he had a friendly, engaging manner and an easy laugh. He had tremendous empathy and believed that he had seen a great deal of injustice over the years. He wanted the justice system to do what it was supposed to do, and he struggled to protect the rights of his clients. Larry had the courage to speak out when he knew that wrong was wrong.

Melissa Hunt Sublett, also known as "Missy," grew up in a stable, working-class area. She had parents whose marriage was intact and who loved their child like parents do. Mattison and Shirley Sublett struggled to help their daughter, whose addiction to drugs plagued her young life. At age twenty-nine, she had been arrested nearly thirty times for prostitution and drugs. She served two terms of incarceration in the Marysville State Penitentiary, but her addiction to crack cocaine was so powerful that she could not overcome it, even after a prison sentence. She married Brian D. Hunt and had three children: Eric, Brandon and Rhiannon. Estranged from her husband, she was living with her parents when she told her mother that she was going for a walk. She never came home. A friend once said of her, "She wouldn't hurt anyone."

William "Bill" Ketler was a solid man. He served as an officer on a small police force in a small town, Copley, Ohio. Of average height and build, he had a shock of thick, slightly unruly, dark hair and a slow, soft smile. Low-key and conscientious, he was married and had a loving family. He was comfortable with his life and his work. Ketler had a fundamental decency that inspired trust.

Stephanie Williams was dealt a difficult hand. Her mother was a prostitute and drug user. Her grandmother sold drugs, and both women's lives were drenched with poverty and violence. Stephanie lived what she learned. She was resentful of her mother and her neglect during Stephanie's childhood. She lived in an environment of drug use, violence and day-to-day survival. Stephanie had little use for men and chose the company of women. She had been arrested for drug crimes and sent to prison. She had a reputation as a bully.

Charles Kirkwood was chief of the Criminal Division in the Summit County Prosecutor's Office in the 1970s. He was a large man, energetic and surprisingly light on his feet for his size. He reminded me of "Rumpole of the Bailey." He was not particular about his appearance and wore inexpensive suits, badly fitted, giving him a perpetually dumpy look. But he was intelligent, and his knowledge of criminal law was exceptional. Juries liked him, and he had the ability to zero in on the critical issues where a case could be won or lost. He was a Democrat who left the Prosecutor's Office when his boss lost reelection. In 1981, he took a position as a law professor with the University of Akron School of Law. He flourished in academia, was highly respected and was named Professor of the Year in 1983. He left the law school in 1994.

Julie Anne Bishop was the owner of the escort business SkyeProm. She was ambitious, hardworking and naïve. Her husband and her mother both worked for SkyeProm. Julie Anne saw herself as a sharp businesswoman. She had made decisions that she thought would protect her from the consequences of the sex trade. She tried to use ordinary business procedures that would give her the appearance of running a legitimate business that was something other than what it actually was.

Katherine Shue was an escort who used the stage name "Angie." She was twenty-three years old and wafer thin, with the complexion of a Kleenex and a mop of occasionally blond hair. Shue was not very successful in her profession. She was frequently homeless, sleeping on couches wherever she could. She used drugs recreationally and was usually short of money. She had worked for several different escort services before joining SkyeProm. She had no loyalty to her boss or to the other women she knew working at SkyeProm. When she was about to be arrested for prostitution, she was more than eager to use what she knew to get herself out of a jam, although that meant throwing everyone at SkyeProm under the bus.

Laura Ridenour was the owner of Touch of Class, a competitor escort service. She was intelligent, self-possessed and worldly. A shapely blonde with lovely, even features, she appeared cool and sophisticated. She was unmarried and had no children. She ran her business efficiently and profitably. She was under no illusions about working in the sex trade.

PROSTITUTION GETS A PROMOTION

J udge, we got the case."

I looked up. Jill Coleman, my bailiff, stood in the doorway to my chambers. "What case?"

"The one with all the escorts. It is big. There are thirty-five defendants. Haven't you heard about it?"

As usual, I was the last to hear anything in the courthouse. "No, I haven't."

"Every defense lawyer in the county will be lining up. Some of the defendants have counsel already, but we'll have to sort out conflicts and make appointments."

"Escorts? What are the charges?"

"Promoting prostitution. Money laundering. The press is going to be all over this. Oh, there's cops too."

A sinking feeling hit my gut. There were few things worse than a police officer as a criminal defendant. "Please get me a copy of the indictment. I need to get an idea of what this is all about."

That was the beginning. Of course, I had no inkling that this case would ravage reputations and end careers, friendships and marriages. I couldn't know then that the pain, embarrassment and antagonism would ripple across the community and the justice system, lasting long after the case officially ended. I came to understand that the true beginning was CenTac.

CenTac is Central Tactical Unit. It is necessary to understand what CenTac was and how it operated. It was created as part of the "War on Drugs" in 1987. The concept was to deploy a separate group of officers that focused on drug trafficking investigations across multiple jurisdictions. The officers and sheriff's deputies in the unit came from every police force in the county, and they worked as a team, sharing information, conducting investigations and coordinating prosecution. CenTac had a governing board, with the county sheriff as chair. The county prosecutor sat on the board and assigned one assistant prosecutor to advise and handle CenTac cases. Police chiefs from various municipalities sat on the board. The feds were participating too, despite their usual disdain for local law enforcement. They had a non-voting seat on the board.

The investigation of drug activity usually requires undercover officers. They befriend, recruit and use informants, establish secret hideouts and buy drugs under surveillance. For CenTac, the goal was to reach the well-protected kingpins at the top and break up high-volume delivery networks. Too often, ordinary police work resulted in just picking up street sellers and drug users, but this has little or no impact on the distribution of narcotics.

The basic idea behind a unit such as CenTac was sound. Individual police departments are limited by the boundaries of the city in which they work, but drug dealing knowns no such boundaries. The sale of narcotics operated in a hierarchy, with sophisticated importation of heroin, cocaine and amphetamines internationally and across distribution networks within the United States. The big money was at the top of the hierarchy, with lesser profits being made farther on down; the final consumer, the user, paid the bill. If CenTac had stayed in the drug business as it was intended to, the Escort Case would never have happened.

Funding for the "War on Drugs" was available through the Ohio Office of Criminal Justice Services. Upon application, CenTac received grant funds for operating expenses. However, a second source of income for CenTac was also developed and became very lucrative. This was forfeiture.

After a successful criminal prosecution, certain laws permitted forfeiture. The judge in the case held a hearing and determined if cash or property were used in or resulted from the commission of the crime. If so, the judge would order that the money go to the state, and then the money would be distributed to the police agencies that developed the case. There was a devil in this detail. The police began to see certain crimes as profit centers. Budgets were often lean, and funds for equipment, vehicles and supplies were always in short supply. But forfeited money could be used to make up what tax money did not provide. I am sure that no police chief would admit that a certain type of case was pursued because the department needed a new paddy wagon. But police officers are subject to the same motivations as everyone else. The state legislatures created these for-profit cases, and savvy law enforcement officers took advantage.

When CenTac made a case that resulted in a forfeiture, the money went first to CenTac. High-level drug busts could involve very significant amounts of money. This provided a definite incentive to pursue cases where large amounts of drugs and money would be involved. Once the money went into CenTac's account, there were guidelines for how it was to be used. But the cash sloshed around quite a bit.

CenTac cases were often complicated because they covered long periods of time in multiple locations and could involve dozens of defendants. To induce a guilty plea, the prosecutor offered to reduce charges in exchange for possible testimony against other defendants and relinquishment of money. When this tactic is used, there is no hearing before a judge, and it isn't necessary to prove that the money is connected to the crime. Money itself becomes a negotiating tool.

When money comes in the door, justice can often go out the window. Investigations that began with suspicions of drug dealing morphed into something else when cash and other valuable assets appeared. This became a template for CenTac cases. Forfeited property was sold, or if cash was forfeited, it was simply deposited in CenTac's account. The various participating police departments were to share the money. Dividing up the cash became a point of contention, and disagreements over the allocation of forfeited money festered. The forfeited money had to be used first to pay CenTac's operating expenses. Money was spent for purchasing equipment and cars, making drug buys and keeping informants happy. Some was spent for drug education.

Another concern was CenTac's independence. Police departments exist as well-regulated hierarchies with a military-style chain of command and reporting and recordkeeping requirements. But CenTac operated outside the normal boundaries needed for good policing and transparency. The CenTac officers, assigned by their individual police departments, went to work in a different environment under a much looser set of controls. Each member of the board that ran the unit was involved in his own professional obligations that demanded his time. They all had work to do beyond just CenTac. Within the unit there was no clear chain of command, and when everybody is responsible, no one is.

CenTac and the for-profit prosecution system it nurtured were humming right along and ready for the next big thing. Prostitution was about to go big time. All that was needed was a slight push to send the dominoes over. Along came Jack Porter and the action began.

A SQUARE PEG IN A ROUND HOLE

I am convinced the Escort Case only became the Escort Case because of Jack Porter. An Akron policeman, Porter started as an entry-level patrolman and worked his way up to the rank of lieutenant. He was not the stereotypical police officer. He questioned authority, was a nonconformist and accepted people as he found them. Porter enjoyed life on his own terms. Lean and attractive to women, he had an active social life, drinking in the bars in the Portage Lakes. The Portage Lakes area developed a reputation for laidback fun where liquor flowed and the attitude was "live and let live."

In keeping with his personality, Porter was lead singer in the rock band Sgt. Jack's Nightwatch. The band played in those same bars at the Portage Lakes where Porter frequently drank. The band also played at civic events, political fundraisers for elected officials and at private parties. They were good musicians. Porter might have gone into music as a career, but he enjoyed working as a police officer. Still, his lifestyle alienated many others on the police force. As one officer stated, "He is a different duck. He is a square peg in a round hole. Not for bad, but he just didn't fit."

Jack Porter's police performance record was spotty in his early years on the force. Generally, it was just his attitude toward supervisors and the length of his hair that earned him reviews of "needs improvement." But overall, his supervisors reviewed him as "very good or outstanding." In 1996, Porter was appointed head of the Akron Vice Squad. The Vice Squad covered the criminal territory occupied by gambling, liquor sales and prostitution. Working Vice put Porter on the streets and usually out

Jack Porter head shot, May 2, 1999. *Jocelyn Williams,* Akron Beacon Journal.

of uniform. He didn't really consider his suspects to be actual criminals and certainly not a serious threat to the good citizens of Akron. In his own words, "With Vice, it's almost like we're dealing with sinners rather than hardened criminals, which to me means that anybody could be involved."

Police Chief Larry Givens put Porter in the job of Vice Squad commander. Givens had known Porter for years, and the men had occasional conflict. Givens had the chance to explain his choice of Porter when he was interviewed by Bob Dyer of the *Akron Beacon Journal.* At that time, in May 1999, Givens was no longer chief but rather served as a member of Summit County Council. "Jack certainly marched to his own drummer, but he was a good police officer." Givens told Dyer. "Through the years, nobody has had more disagreements with Jack Porter," said Givens. "I mean, we've yelled at each other. But I tell you what—we always did our jobs. As a police officer, I would go on a call with him and I would trust him with my life."

In Vice, Porter often worked with Officer Don Fulkerson. Fulkerson had grown up in Akron wanting to be a police officer. He was quiet, earnest and respected both in the community and by his fellow officers. He was a family man, married with four children. He loved being a police officer. He was in many ways the polar opposite of Jack Porter, but sometimes those opposites do attract. Porter was older and more experienced, and he led Fulkerson down roads he would otherwise never have traveled.

Porter's work on Vice brought him into the underworld of prostitution. The consensual sale of sex by adults constitutes prostitution. It is illegal in Ohio, but individual attitudes about it vary dramatically. Some consider it immoral, while others view it as merely a nuisance or possibly dangerous. Still others consider it the oldest profession, an inevitable part of life, nobody's business and no problem whatsoever. But whatever their opinion, most people find it fascinatingly taboo. A wildly popular romantic comedy in 1990 was the film *Pretty Woman,* starring Richard Gere and Julia Roberts. A wealthy businessman hires a hard-luck prostitute as his escort. There is no doubt that the relationship includes sex for money, as the two negotiate their respective requirements. With a production budget of only $14 million, the film saw a box office gross of $463.4 million.

Prostitution to the ordinary person conjures up the "street walker." This is usually a freelance sex worker who may or may not have a man who "protects" her and takes the money she receives. He is her "pimp." While a pimp may have two or more women working the streets and providing him money, this is not an organized operation. It is usually an exploitative and abusive relationship that essentially enslaves the women. Some women are true freelancers, working where and when they choose and keeping the money they receive. Too often their "profession" has been chosen to support drug addiction. It becomes a destructive cycle of degradation and physical and mental deterioration. An old saying sums this up: "She is more to be pitied than censored."

"Escorts," as a thin cover for sex workers, have been around for a long time. In 1998, Akron had several businesses providing this service. Two were Touch of Class and Skye Promotions, known as SkyeProm. They competed for clients and for employees. Each provided client referrals and transportation for the women who worked for them. Each accepted cash, checks or credit cards for payment and processed the charges through the banks as any other credit transaction. The companies charged service fees and paid the women with payroll checks as any employer would. In an effort to avoid the illegality of the enterprise, each company used contracts of employment that specified the women were not providing sexual contact for money but were dancing or providing companionship. In the business, providing sexual intercourse was referred to as "full service" or being "open minded."

None of the women employed as escorts used their real names. They selected a "working" name, a stage name: Summer, April, Autumn, Jasmine, Ashley, Dee, Tiffany, Barbi, Sassy, Amber, Tyler, Angie, Brandy, Skye, Talli, Star, Heidi, Tammy, Korena, Flora, Nicole, Aimee, Holly, Missy, Carmen, Kyleigh and more. Some women worked only as escorts, but many of the women had other jobs: respiratory therapist, nursing student, waitress, dancer, bank collections supervisor and a psychology major at the University of Akron who "wants to help people." They weren't all women. One male escort used the name "Christian." I suspect the stage names enabled the escorts to take a step away from what they were doing, to put some distance between the job and the person who did it.

The businesses were run by women. Laura Ridenour operated Touch of Class, and Julie Anne Bishop ran SkyeProm. Julie Anne's husband, Joseph Bishop, was also involved, as was her mother, Olga Joseph. Laura Ridenour employed her friend Wendy Thrasher Moats. The escorts worked for one or more of the local services, and the different businesses offered a variety of services. Each escort decided what she would and would not do. When a potential client contacted an escort service, the receptionist who took the call asked the client to specify what particular service he was requesting. Then the decision was made to refer a specific escort who was willing to fulfill the request. If an individual escort was "open minded" and would provide a wide variety of services, she would get more referrals than one who was less willing. Escorts were paid based on the number of referrals they got and their flexibility regarding the specific services they offered. A fee schedule was established for each type of activity, and the women received tips. Business was doing just fine when Lieutenant Jack Porter of the Vice Squad arrived in January 1996.

Porter had been working in Vice for a year and a half when, in September 1997, Akron police chief Edward Irvine received an anonymous letter attacking Porter. Anonymous letters are the first choice of cowards, but when they allege police wrongdoing, they cannot be ignored. This letter alleged several instances of misconduct by Porter and appeared to have been written by someone within the police department. Normally when such a situation arises, an investigation by a separate unit, Internal Affairs Investigations, begins. However, the anonymous letter writer claimed that the two Internal Affairs investigators had a close personal relationship with Porter that should preclude those officers from investigating him.

So, two other experienced officers, Captain Craig Gilbride and Captain Douglas Prade, were assigned to investigate. They began by interviewing the two Internal Affairs investigators: Lieutenant Elizabeth Daugherty and Lieutenant Paul Calvaruso. The anonymous letter writer claimed that Porter had been observed in public bars playing "Liar's Poker" with them and another officer, Captain Paul Callahan. When questioned, both officers admitted that they played with Porter at the Akron Family Restaurant one time to determine who would pay for dessert. They also stated that the only other time they recalled playing "Liar's Poker" with Porter was five years earlier at Mitch's Lounge during a shift party. Both officers denied knowing of any illegal acts committed by Porter, but they acknowledged that their close personal relationship with him might make it difficult for them to investigate him.

After interviewing the two Internal Affairs investigators, Gilbride and Prade started their own investigation by interviewing the officers in the Vice Squad. Each officer was separately taken into the conference room of the chief of police and asked a series of questions about Vice operations, procedures, accounting for money and time, morale, leaks that affected undercover operations and specific questions about Jack Porter.

The first topic they explored was the writer's claim that Porter left work to play golf by taking "time due," which was undocumented. This went nowhere. Vice had no set procedures for logging "time due" and no evidence that he played golf without logging it on the daily detail. The next claim concerned Porter's alleged conflict of interest by playing with his band at the same liquor establishments he was supposed to police. Vault 328, a bar in downtown Akron, was given as an example. Gilbride and Prade dismissed the claim, finding no evidence, although they noted he primarily played at establishments outside the city of Akron.

The next allegation was that Porter publicly socialized with a known escort whose identity was not stated. Supposedly, Porter gave her information that compromised a Vice Squad investigation. The investigators assumed that this referred to Wendy Thrasher Moats. But the allegation was rejected since they found no corroboration and only speculation.

A more serious allegation concerned a known escort Porter brought into the off-site Vice Squad office. One of the most important aspects of undercover work is to conceal the actual identities of undercover officers. If an undercover officer becomes known as a police officer, he is no longer effective. He also faces danger if the suspects he is investigating know who he really is. Members of the Vice Squad went to considerable effort to conceal their identities. They maintained an off-site location to go to and complete reports, meet with other officers and do investigative work.

Officers often worked with confidential informants (CIs) who provided information and assisted in actual arrests in return for avoiding criminal charges or getting plea reductions if charged. But although a CI may be working with an officer, these people were part of a community and had friends and associates who were likely involved in criminal activity. Knowing who was working as an undercover officer was not likely to remain confidential for long.

Porter allegedly brought Laura Ridenour into the off-site office when undercover officers were working. Ridenour owned Touch of Class. Porter, when asked by the investigators, acknowledged that she was a CI but did not remember bringing her to the office. He did admit bringing Marchelle Davis into the office on one occasion, an action verified by officers present. Marchelle Davis was working as a confidential informant when he took her to the off-site office. The investigators found it probable that he took both women to the off-site office. This allegation was now the first charge against Porter.

Another allegation was that Porter compromised an ongoing gambling investigation when he went into a bar and attempted to place a bet with a suspected bookie. When the bet was refused, he became angry and told the man that he was the Vice Squad commander and he was going to "get" him. Porter admitted doing this while one of his own officers sat working undercover at the end of the bar. He defended himself by saying that the investigation had gone as far as it could without any bets actually being placed. So he tried to place a bet, and when denied, Porter confronted the bartender and the owner. But he neglected to tell his own officer of his plan. Gilbride and Prade determined that his actions were not ideal but that it was more of a misunderstanding with his officer than error.

Next they looked at the claim that Porter accepted free trips to Las Vegas, compliments of a convicted drug felon. No evidence supported the claim, and Porter denied it. Then they considered the allegation that Porter's system for accounting for Vice Squad funds was "loose" and should be audited. However, an audit had previously been ordered for an unrelated reason, and the auditor found all funds in order and accounted for. The final issue raised by the letter was that Porter, as the assigned liaison with the Akron Board of Education, failed to attend meetings with the board or, basically, do the job. When asked if Porter failed to do his job, members of the board of education and its employees said no. They also stated that he attended meetings and was available when needed. Porter's work was satisfactory. So each of these claims died a quiet death.

This could have been the end of the internal investigation triggered by the anonymous letter. The two investigators had the option of reporting back to the chief that only two of the allegations had merit. But they chose another path. In the words of the investigating officers, "Although these allegations are serious in nature, more troubling issues were uncovered during the course of the investigation. These issues go to the very heart of the ethics and integrity expected of an undercover unit. While interviewing detectives assigned to the Vice Squad, a number of concerns and allegations surfaced."

The first incident, considered the most serious by the officers, I refer to as the "Showdown at the Best Western Motel." As is typical in many prostitution investigations, an escort service is contacted to send an escort to a specific location for a client who is, in fact, an undercover police officer. The officer meets the escort in a motel room and tries to arrange a "deal" exchanging sexual conduct for an agreed amount of money. Without the deal, no crime is committed and no arrest can be made. The negotiation of this deal produces the most farcical aspect of these cases.

The officers and the escorts know that if the escort does not explicitly state what she is willing to do and for how much, she cannot be arrested. Also, the deal must be made before any sexual contact occurs because the officers may not engage in sexual acts with the women. The women use a common ploy—hinting and using euphemisms that can later be argued to have multiple meanings. When an officer posing as a client asks what he will get for his money, an escort might say, "What you get on the first night of your honeymoon," "If you like it, you can give me a tip" or "I have to charge you an agency fee, but anything over that you can decide but my time is worth $100." If the officer presses for something more specific, she may tell him what she will do but not for how much. Or she may specify an amount but promise a "massage" or a "lap dance" while naked, which can later be argued as not constituting sexual conduct.

In all fairness, the law in this area is not extremely helpful in giving guidance to the officers. The Vice Squad had no internal policy about what the officers could and could not do. Officers also use their own discretion in deciding if the arrest should be made. Whatever they decide, the case has to be proven in court. Some judges are very accepting of what will satisfy the elements needed to prove the offense. Others are sticklers for specific language or particular acts before they will find a crime occurred. Because soliciting offenses are misdemeanors and not high on the priority of criminal acts, these cases are very rarely tried by a jury. It is also very uncommon for the case to go to trial at all since guilty pleas and paying fines avoid publicity.

This particular investigation at the Best Western involved several officers and two rooms with an adjoining door. According to Detective Richard Oldaker, the operation was an escort sting. They called one of the agencies and asked for an escort to be sent to a specific room at the Best Western Motel. Sergeant Tom Kelly and Jack Porter stayed in one room, while Oldaker, Detective Humphrey and Detective Hudnall stayed in the adjoining room. Oldaker observed a blond woman wearing a red dress arrive, accompanied by a driver. The woman entered the room occupied by Kelly and Porter. The driver waited outside the door.

Seeing a man outside the door, Oldaker thought that this may be a "rip off." This would be essentially a theft of the money provided by the client without any "services" being provided. So Oldaker went to the adjoining door to listen. Kelly left the room. Oldaker thought the woman got paid $100 just for showing up. The woman asked Porter how he got her number, and he said he got it from a newspaper. Oldaker heard a sound that he thought was a zipper being unzipped and then some talk about a condom and, later, moaning. Then he heard the woman ask "Here, do you want a washcloth to clean up with?" She asked for some mouthwash, but she said if there was no mouthwash, she would have a beer. There was beer in the room. Porter asked about his friend. She gave him her pager number and said he could call her later. She said it would be another $100 for her current services, which is what he gave her, and she left the room. She was observed meeting the man outside in the parking lot, and they drove away.

Oldaker told the other two officers what he had heard, and then the three officers entered the room. Oldaker confronted Porter. He claimed that he gave Porter some Kleenex, and Porter said, "What is this for?" Oldaker answered, "Want a washcloth to clean up with?" Porter then accused them of listening through the door. Oldaker said Porter stated that the woman had unzipped his pants and placed her mouth on his penis, but he stopped her. He said he needed a washcloth to remove her lipstick from his thighs and genitals.

Porter had a slightly different rendition when he was asked during the internal investigation. He claimed that after she came into the room, she got $100 and immediately gave the money to the man outside the door. Porter said he had never seen that done before. Then she asked what he wanted, and he finally said a "blow job." She unzipped his pants. He said that he kept trying to talk about a deal, but she wouldn't talk and started kissing his thighs and genitals. He said she wore bright-red lipstick, which was getting all over him. Porter said, "We have to take care of my buddy and I've got lipstick all over me." She offered to get him a washcloth to clean up. She then gave him her pager number and said it would be another $100 for her to come back later. He said they would page her and gave her $190. She left. Porter said he couldn't make an arrest because there was no deal. He denied that she ever touched his penis. He said she left with $190 of the Vice Squad's money. However, while she personally got $190, the Vice Squad was out $290.

Gilbride and Prade believed that there was probable cause to conclude that Porter received oral sex from the unknown escort at the Best Western. They also were concerned that there was no paperwork on file regarding this investigation and no documentation regarding the amount of money spent, the escort service called or the name of the woman who responded.

A follow-up investigation was done by Captain Gilbride after the arrest of Theresa Frescki. Frescki told Gilbride that she ran a small escort service known as Lace Escorts. She stated that she received a call at the service and agreed to meet two men at the Gilchrist Road Best Western Motel. She said she went to the motel, where she masturbated and performed oral sex on a white male. After her arrest a short time later for soliciting, she learned that the white male was Lieutenant Jack Porter.

Another aspect of the investigation involved Porter's relationship with Laura Ridenour. According to Porter, Ridenour was assisting in an investigation of a man named Mark Bell. Porter thought that Bell had beaten several escorts and stolen from them. Ridenour had helped as a decoy in an unsuccessful sting operation to apprehend Bell, but Bell failed to show. Vice had specific procedures for the use of information sources, but Porter did not follow them with Laura Ridenour. He had no case file to indicate when he met with her, where the meetings took place or what information was provided. Further, it was against city policy to have private citizens used as decoys in undercover police operations because of liability issues. Ridenour had been to the off-site Vice office, compromising the identity and safety of the officers. The two investigators found these allegations credible and serious.

Gilbride and Prade also found that Porter used Wendy Thrasher Moats, another escort who worked for Ridenour, as an information source over an extended period of time without documentation and without the information source procedure being followed. Porter's relationship with Moats was an issue. In his interview with the investigators, another vice officer, Officer Rodney Criss, stated that Wendy Thrasher Moats lived in an apartment below his girlfriend at 90 Merriman Road. He had never seen Jack Porter at her apartment and didn't know what kind of car Porter drove. Criss stated that he had talked to Moats several months before, regarding a sign he observed in the basement of the building. The sign was from Lisa's Cabaret, a bar with live professional dancing. Criss asked Moats if she worked there, and she said she had worked there in the past. She said "Capt. Jack" had given her the sign. Criss assumed she meant Porter. Moats also told Criss that she had dated Porter on several occasions.

The officers looked into other allegations that Porter had compromised cases involving gambling at MaGoo's Lounge and J.D.'s Lounge because of his relationship with the owners. Eventually, the investigators recommended disciplinary actions for each of the violations ranging from reprimand to dismissal. In their report, they concluded, "Irrespective of what the administration deems appropriate discipline in this matter, the investigating officers feel it is imperative that Porter be administratively transferred from the Vice Squad. The level of suspicion and distrust is such that keeping him in this unit would be a major mistake." The internal investigation report was forwarded to Police Chief Edward Irvine, who began disciplinary proceedings that could result in Porter being fired.

By January 1998, Jack Porter had hired a lawyer, Tom Adgate. Adgate shared much of Jack's outlook on life. His own past had been troubled. He had faced serious emotional problems and self-medicated with alcohol. But he had found his way out of the despair of addiction with the help of AA and created a good life. Happily married and with a successful law practice, he offered help to everyone who reached out for it. His compassion, intelligence and terrific sense of humor made him an effective lawyer. Tom didn't judge—he empathized and was there to help.What better lawyer for Jack Porter?

The stakes were high for Porter. Losing his pension after his many years of service on the force would be a disaster. Despite his love for his profession, Jack Porter voluntarily resigned from the Akron Police Department on January 12, 1998, retaining his pension. On January 15, 1998, the Akron Vice Squad and CenTac began considering a joint investigation into the escort services in Summit County.

RICO MEETS THE ESCORTS

With Jack Porter's resignation from the Akron Police Department, significant changes began to take place in the Vice Squad. No longer were Laura Ridenour and her escort service, Touch of Class, "off-limits." The decision had to be made whether to expand the investigation of the escort services and to do so in connection with CenTac. This would bring more officers into the investigations, expand the jurisdictions in which they could work and increase the money available for the investigation. An assistant Summit County prosecutor would be assigned to develop the individual cases and take them to the grand jury for indictments.

However, this presented a significant problem. The investigation of prostitution lay outside the intended scope of CenTac's work, which was to reduce illegal drug sales. CenTac's grant money was for this purpose and this purpose only. But this might not turn out to be a major stumbling block because drug use and sales occasionally were part of transactions involving prostitution. It could credibly be claimed that the drug offenses were part of the escort services. Once again, the potential profitability of a criminal case would be used to escalate the charges from low-level misdemeanors and felonies to significant felonies with provisions for forfeiture.

The CenTac governing board included County Prosecutor Maureen O'Connor. She had served as a Summit County Common Pleas judge from 1993 until being appointed as county prosecutor in 1995. Why would a judge resign to become a prosecutor? Being a judge is a high-status position. You are seen as an important person who is by definition honorable and honest.

But judges have very little actual power. A judge doesn't have patronage to reward others with jobs. Judges do not initiate cases. They wait passively to be randomly assigned a case. They impose sentences but only within a range imposed by the legislature. For someone who is aggressive and ambitious, being a judge is not a satisfying profession.

Maureen O'Connor was aggressive and ambitious. When the opportunity came to take the job of county prosecutor, she didn't hesitate. She also didn't hesitate when CenTac sought to convert ordinary low-level crimes into major offenses with forfeitures. These cases provided publicity and demonstrated to a naïve public how tough the prosecutor was. O'Connor was the primary person who should have provided a professional assessment of the requirements of justice. Do the defendants deserve to be charged with serious major offenses? Does this provide protection for the community and serve as a deterrent to similar criminal acts? Should the resources of the justice system best be used for such a prosecution? When these kinds of questions are not asked and considered, the consequences can be damaging to individuals and affect the community as a whole. The job of the prosecutor is to do justice, not to exploit the system for money and publicity.

Considering its mission is drug enforcement, should CenTac begin a joint investigation with the Akron Vice Squad? This wasn't drug trafficking. As the prosecutor and the lawyer on the CenTac Board, Maureen O'Connor was in the position to decide whether CenTac should investigate prostitution. The decision was made early in 1998 that CenTac should and would begin a joint investigation with the Akron Vice Squad. This had the potential for becoming a high-profile case with plenty of publicity. All of this could be useful to Prosecutor O'Connor. Without that decision, the Escort Case would never have begun its reign of destruction.

To become the Summit County prosecutor, O'Connor resigned as a judge in 1995. This created a vacancy, and when a vacancy occurs in an Ohio Common Pleas Court, the governor appoints someone to fill the seat until the next election. This is a highly partisan process, and local politicians usually make the actual selection. So it was in Summit County. Michael Callahan was serving as an Akron municipal judge, and he was ambitious. A move to Common Pleas Court was a step up in status and salary. Callahan was appointed to take O'Connor's seat on the court.

CenTac was composed of officers from every police department in the county and included deputy sheriffs. Its organization was not as tight as a police department, but it followed standard investigative practices. When a team of officers takes action in furtherance of an investigation, the leading

Judith Bandy. *From the* Akron Beacon Journal.

officer writes a report and submits it to his superior, making it available for other involved officers to review. Effective investigations require information sharing. If an officer records an interview as part of his report, it is transcribed, and the transcript is also filed and available. Reports of this kind are called a Report of Investigation, or ROI. It provides the date and place of the incident, the subject, arrests made (if any), all relevant facts and the name of the officer making the report; it includes a narrative that starts with a synopsis of what happened and who was involved. An ongoing investigation may have dozens of ROIs involving the various actions taken, physical evidence noted and the suspects identified. If a report is recorded on tape, transcriptions are made, indexed and filed.

Prosecutor O'Connor selected an assistant criminal prosecutor to work on the cases that CenTac developed. She assigned Judith Bandy, usually referred to as Judie. Judie was smart, disciplined, intense and devoted to law enforcement. She firmly believed that she was working on the side of the angels, and she did so with complete commitment. She thrived on complex cases with hundreds of documents, multiple defendants and lengthy indictments. She spent hours and hours in her office organizing evidence, reviewing reports and interviewing witnesses. Although married, she had no children, and her dedication to her job kept her in the office evenings and weekends. Thin to the point of being gaunt, she seemed to live on coffee and cigarettes. She wore severely tailored suits but no jewelry or makeup—she was all business. The police loved her.

Defense lawyers did not. Their primary issue concerned their collective belief that she routinely withheld evidence. In Ohio, a prosecutor is required to provide to the defense all reports, statements, witnesses and materials that are relevant to the charges in the case. In some areas, this process begins with a motion by the defense and production of documents and evidence in writing by the prosecutor. But in Summit County, the prosecutor developed a system known as "open file discovery." Every defendant had a file in the prosecutor's office. These files were available for inspection by defense lawyers. They could look at the file and take notes but could not make copies of anything in the files unless the prosecutor gave permission.

A prosecutor could withhold filing evidence until after a defense attorney had come in and examined the file. Then, shortly before trial, the additional evidence would appear in the file, sometimes just hours before the trial began. Judie Bandy was famous for this. When challenged, she inevitably responded that she continuously worked her cases and only just discovered the late evidence. Depending on the nature of the evidence, the judge might continue the trial if it would be materially unfair to the defense to proceed. However, a defense lawyer's client, sitting in jail and anxious for the trial to start, might urge the attorney to go forward anyway. Witnesses were subpoenaed, and everyone was ready to go. Under those circumstances, the defense lawyers declined to delay the trial, although they frequently felt that they had been handled.

Another complaint was that Bandy would not settle a case by plea bargain unless the police agreed to it. She was not alone; this was common practice in the Summit County Prosecutor's Office. However, good practice dictates that offering a plea to reduced charges should be a decision made only by the prosecutor. A good prosecutor evaluates the strength of the evidence, what defense is being offered, how a jury is likely to react and how the victim may feel. The prosecutor should consider what other charges may be legally appropriate given the evidence and whether a plea bargain would be in the interest of justice. The plea bargain is offered and presented to the defense and must be accepted or rejected by the defendant. It may or may not include a sentence recommendation to the judge. The defense lawyer can recommend that the client accept or refuse the offer, but whether to accept it or not rests solely with the defendant. A guilty plea may not be coerced. It must be knowingly, intelligently and voluntarily given.

The balance of power in the justice system is important; it ensures that all facts and circumstances are considered and that each of the three participants acts within his or her own sphere of authority. The prosecutor is the pivotal role in the system and has the most power. Giving police the power to approve or disapprove a proposed plea bargain distorts the discretion a prosecutor should exercise and infringes on the independence a prosecutor must have. It simply gives the police power they should not have. Once an investigation ends and the charges decided by the grand jury, the work of the police is complete except as they may be called to testify at a trial or unless new evidence comes to light.

"Got it?" *Chip Bok,* Akron Beacon Journal.

Officers should not have the power to tell defendants that they can send them to prison or that they can determine the outcome of the case. This is a coercive power, easily abused. Only an attorney should have the authority to determine the legal issues and what justice requires. Judie Bandy's strong relationship with the police arose partly from her deference to the police in the resolution of her cases. But they also knew of her dedication and incredible work ethic.

CenTac certainly did not intend to investigate simple prostitution cases. The unit needed bigger fish to fry. It also needed money for operations. To get that money, it needed cases with assets that could be forfeited. The real money was in the escort services as actual businesses. So the focus shifted to the two largest, Touch of Class and SkyeProm. This is where the RICO charges could be brought.

These cases required more than individual stings for the sale of sex. They needed evidence to support charges of serious felonies with forfeiture potential: engaging in a pattern of corrupt activity, conspiracy to engage in a pattern of corrupt activity, promoting prostitution and money laundering. These were the classic charges known as RICO—Racketeer Influenced and Corrupt Organizations Act—originally a federal criminal construct for racketeering in criminal organizations, popularly known as organized crime, the rackets or the syndicates. Legislators recognized that crimes were often not standalone thefts or assaults. They involved several well-organized actors who used much more sophisticated methods than the drug seller on the street. RICO charges provided for forfeitures. States adopted their own RICO statutes using the federal model. CenTac wanted RICO charges for the forfeitures they could provide. Any drug activity they encountered would be gravy.

OPERATION RED LIGHT

By January 15, 1998, the new joint CenTac unit had set up the first sting. It called the ongoing investigation Operation Red Light. It set this sting at the Comfort Inn in Copley, Ohio. Again, Detective Richard Oldaker was the undercover officer. He placed a call to Touch of Class and arranged for a woman to come to the motel. That evening, at 9:33 p.m., "Autumn" arrived. CenTac detectives were in an adjoining room listening through a wire recording on an audio tape. "Autumn" was Wendy Thrasher Moats.

After some cagey negotiations, both Oldaker and Moats were naked. Following some preliminaries, she asked him to put on a condom. He did. She began performing oral sex, which was started and then aborted when he said the condom was painful. She said she was sorry but she couldn't do anything without the condom. He paid her a total of $350 cash, which included the $50 service fee due the agency. She left, got into her car and drove away. She was followed by detectives to a home on Falmouth Road in Fairlawn, Ohio, the home of Laura Ridenour. Moats went into the residence and then came out with a small child. Officers followed her to her own home, an

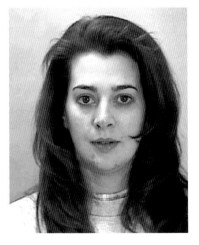

Wendy Thrasher Moats. *File photo mug shot.*

"Escort" knocking on motel door. *Bruce Ford, photographed June 2021.*

apartment building on Merriman Road in Akron. The officers assumed that she gave the $50 service fee to Ridenour. They made no arrest but noted that she would be arrested when a warrant was signed. The joint unit continued setting up stings and developing cases without making arrests.

On March 11, 1998, Summit County deputy Kelly L. Fatheree reported information she received from Summit County deputy Larry Limbert. Limbert said he received a telephone call from an unknown woman who identified herself as "Talli." Talli gave Limbert the following account. Talli stated that she met Lieutenant Porter and Sergeant Fulkerson in October or November 1997 when she worked for Laura Ridenour. Talli said that during her employment with Touch of Class, she helped with an investigation that Lieutenant Porter and Sergeant Fulkerson were working on concerning Mark Bell, an escort client who allegedly would assault escorts. Talli stated that during the investigation, she, Laura Ridenour, Lieutenant Porter and Sergeant Fulkerson went to the White Rino (bar) in Portage Lakes and got "trashed." Talli stated that she and Lieutenant Porter left the White Rino, went to a secluded spot and had sex in the back seat of his undercover vehicle. She said that Laura and Sergeant Fulkerson left the White Rino and went to Laura's residence on Killian Road. Talli added that Laura would see Sergeant Fulkerson on a regular basis.

On May 15, 1998, Deputy Kelly Fatheree conducted an extensive interview with Talli. Talli identified numerous people working in various escort services and gave their addresses and information about them. She provided the names and addresses of clients. The two women made several calls to the escort services inquiring about work, each recorded as evidence. Fatheree continued working with Talli developing information through the month of May.

In June, CenTac decided that Detective David B. Smith from the Cuyahoga Falls Police Department would go undercover and begin driving escorts for SkyeProm. Julie Anne Bishop ran SkyeProm from an office in Cuyahoga Falls, Ohio. The office was used to answer the phone, dispatch escorts and provide a location to service clients when necessary. In order to place Smith as an undercover driver, CenTac rented the office space next door to the SkyeProm office. Smith was set up as the owner of a limousine service, E.L.S. & Associates. CenTac provided a phone and a limousine to drive. He let the escort service know that he was willing to drive the escorts when he was not otherwise working.

On June 17, SkyeProm asked Smith to pick up Lee Metarko and drive her to the Best Western on Gilchrist Road in Akron, which he did. Smith waited at the bar in the motel until Metarko returned and gave him twenty dollars. He gave her several business cards, and she said she would keep him in mind. Over the next several weeks, Smith began to regularly drive various escorts and talked with the women working in the office while he taped discussions with them about the escort operations.

Operation Red Light really lit up during a sting on July 18 when escort "Angie" knocked on the door at the Best Western and Sergeant J. Phister answered. Game on. He introduced himself as Bill Roberts. She didn't request identification and asked what he did for a living. He said he worked for BP Oil and was in town for a meeting. There were BP Oil shirts hanging on a rack as props. She asked where his luggage was. He said it was a one-day event and he traveled light. She inquired what he was looking to do. Phister said that a friend had told him he tried an escort agency and they were a lot of fun. Angie got a big smile on her face and said that she bet he did but that they were not allowed to do that sort of thing. She stated that Vice was really cracking down on escort agencies. Phister told her that what she did would be up to her, meaning going against agency policy. She said the owner could sue her because she signed a contract stating that she would

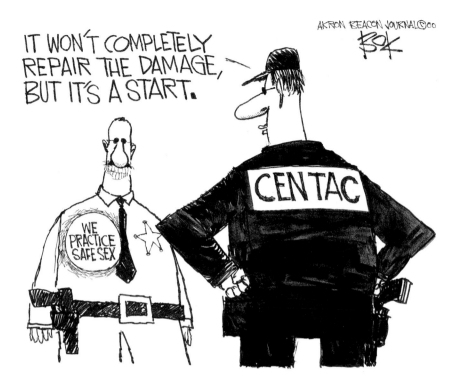

"It won't completely repair the damage, but it's a start." *Chip Bok*, Akron Beacon Journal.

not solicit any customers. Phister asked if Vice was the police. She stated it was and told him there was going to be a big meeting on Tuesday. She expected the owner was going to tell all the girls to cease full-service calls.

Angie then looked at him and asked what he would like to have—"other than getting his socks knocked off." Phister said, "Let's start with a massage." She said she had to collect the service fee money, $90, up front. Phister told her that he did not have the exact amount but that he wasn't worried about change and handed her $100. She stripped down to her bra and panties as he lay on the bed, and then she straddled him and began to massage his back. She told him that she had two kids who were in the custody of her ex-husband, and she was trying to get custody back. She stated that she had done a year in jail and was on parole for felony child endangering.

After a few minutes, Phister asked her where they could go next. She said that she could do a nude massage that would be $50 extra for topless and an additional $50 for no bottoms. He got up and gave her another $100. She said she wanted him to go nude to make her feel more comfortable. Phister disrobed and returned to the bed. Angie said now she felt better because she could see that Phister wasn't wearing a wire. She resumed the massage. Phister said to her, "Oh, you are going to get me all hot and bothered and then you are going to leave." She lay down beside him and said that she didn't have a rubber—did he? He said he would check and uselessly searched for a few minutes before saying that he didn't have one and returned to the bed. She told him that she did not swallow and that oral without swallowing would be another $75. Phister said that would be great. He had made his deal, and he got up and signaled for the surveillance officers to come in the room.

He told Angie that he wanted to wash first, and she thanked him for being considerate. He went into the bathroom, stalling until the officers arrived. He went back to the bed with a towel on and informed the naked woman that he was with the Akron Police Vice Unit and that she was under arrest for soliciting. The other officers arrived and conducted an initial interview. Angie answered their questions. The officers considered the possibility of using her to gather information from the inside of the agency. They all agreed and decided to hold off charging her to see what cooperation they could get. Angie agreed to cooperate and started giving them information.

"Angie" was Katherine Shue. She was probably in the wrong profession, although there aren't many alternatives available to a young woman with her skills. She had worked for several different escort services before SkyeProm but could not be considered a success as an escort. She was always short of money, frequently homeless and sleeping on couches wherever she could. She used drugs recreationally and floated through life with no purpose. She was, however, an opportunist. When she was about to be arrested for prostitution, she jumped at the chance to use what she knew to get herself out of a jam. What this would mean for her co-workers wasn't a concern.

She began her job as a confidential informant by telling the officers about the meeting planned for the SkyeProm escorts on Tuesday night, July 21, at the Bob Evans Restaurant in the city of Macedonia at 7:00 p.m. All the employees were required to attend or risk being fired. The meeting's purpose was to discuss the problems with the police regarding soliciting. Shue said that she couldn't be there because she was having surgery but that the owner, Julie Anne Bishop, told her the meeting would be taped; she could go to Bishop's house and listen to the tape. Until she recovered from her surgery, she would only be answering the phone at the office. She offered to wear a wire when she listened to the tape. When asked if Bishop would ever suspect her of wearing a wire, Shue replied that she would not because "Angie" is Julie's number one girl.

Katherine Shue had kept a ledger since April 1998 listing all her clients, dates and whether they paid by cash or credit. She provided the officers with the ledger. She then checked in with the agency by phone to let them know that she was leaving the Best Western. She got ninety dollars to cover the cost of the service call, which she was required to turn over to the agency. She repeated that she would be very willing to work with them on anything they needed to know. When Katherine Shue left the Best Western at 3:15 a.m., she was a confidential informant for CenTac.

On July 21, the business meeting of SkyeProm took place at the Bob Evans. Eight CenTac officers organized extensive surveillance in the restaurant, in the parking lot and at a Knights Inn just south of the restaurant. They set up a video recorder. The officers identified vehicles and individuals and took still photos and videos. The next day, Shue paged Phister and told him that she had information from the agency that she had written down that could be useful. Phister and Detective Andrews met with Shue at Pillitiere's Restaurant, where she provided a list of the stage names, real first names, physical descriptions, phone and pager numbers and some specific information about all of the individuals working at SkyeProm. She discussed relationships between the employees, operations and the fallout from the recent meeting, where two escorts were fired from the agency.

The following day, Katherine Shue again contacted Phister and indicated that she would be going to Berea, Ohio, to the home of Julie Anne Bishop to discuss the recent meeting. They arranged for a wire in her purse so she could transmit the conversation to the officers following in a van. At Bishop's home, Katherine and Julie Anne talked about changes in the agency, which Bishop said would no longer be full service. Escorts would have to use drivers provided by the agency, and Julie Anne herself would assign escorts when calls came in from clients, ostensibly to prevent theft within the agency.

Julie Anne Bishop saw herself as a businesswoman. She was bright and hardworking and wanted to succeed. She set up internal systems to operate her business and tried to convince herself that she was not running a prostitution service because she did not want her girls to be "full service" and had fired a few when she learned what they were doing. The problem was that the clients wanted sex, not just dancing at bachelor parties and giving massages. She knew that, and she knew that "full service" was where the money was. She also knew that her husband was not happy with her business, although the money she brought in supported him and her mother. She struggled with all the usual problems of a small business owner and one more: the police wanted to arrest her employees.

Operation Red Light continued into the fall, with Smith working undercover and driving escorts. But then a new strategy began. Smith contrived to tell Julie Anne Bishop that he knew a businessman in Chicago who wanted to buy SkyeProm. CenTac officers knew that Bishop was frustrated with running the agency. Smith explained that the buyer wanted information about the value of the business, cash flow, bank records and tax returns; in short, just what CenTac needed to prove money laundering and racketeering. Bishop agreed to start getting the information together using her accountant.

On November 10, before Bishop collected all the necessary documentation, Smith suggested that they could sweeten the deal by including Touch of Class as well. SkyeProm's major competitor would vanish, and the surviving agency would significantly increase its revenue. He asked Bishop to meet with Laura Ridenour to see if she would consider selling. They agreed that this would be a better deal for the buyer. Having agreed, they moved on to discuss the SkyeProm Christmas party. Yes, escort businesses have Christmas parties.

Judge Michael Callahan sworn in as Summit County prosecutor. *Ed Suba Jr.*, Akron Beacon Journal.

After January 1, 1999, Bishop contacted Laura Ridenour, who agreed to consider selling Touch of Class as well as her other escort businesses. These she operated under fictitious names but within the Touch of Class organization. A meeting was set at the Sheraton Suites Hotel in Cuyahoga Falls, Ohio, with Bishop, Moats, Ridenour and "Pat Daily" as the undercover buyer. Daily was actually an Internal Revenue Agent from Cleveland. Initially, they could not reach a deal, but both women agreed to provide additional valuation documentation. By this point, CenTac had extensive evidence, including lists of employees and clients, cash receipts, credit card records, bank records, multiple undercover stings waiting for warrants and tape and video recordings.

Then CenTac's governing board underwent a significant change. In November 1998, Maureen O'Connor became lieutenant governor of Ohio. She resigned as Summit County prosecutor, and the local Republican Party appointed as her successor Judge Michael Callahan, who had taken her seat as Summit County judge in the Common Pleas Court. He resigned his judicial seat and was sworn in as Summit County prosecutor on January 25, 1999. Mike Callahan was a large man, red-haired, bearded and proudly Irish. He socialized in bars and had worked as a bouncer during law school. His nickname was "Turk," and he displayed it on a vanity license plate on his car, a dark-blue Cadillac. He married an intelligent, capable woman. Ambitious and confident, he saw the prosecutor's job as a more powerful position than a judgeship.

Shortly before Michael Callahan became prosecutor, Judie Bandy presented the escort cases to the Summit County Grand Jury. None of the individuals whose cases were considered by the grand jury was under arrest or in custody. This type of indictment is referred to as a "direct indictment." Warrants for arrest are issued after the charges have been signed by the grand jury, and only then are the accused apprised that they have been charged with one or more crimes.

The indictments were issued on February 19, 1999. The charges varied slightly from defendant to defendant but included engaging in a pattern of corrupt activity, conspiracy to engage in a pattern of corrupt activity, promoting prostitution, money laundering, obstruction of justice, endangering children, receiving stolen property and trafficking in marijuana. Several charges also had specifications for forfeiture of property. Thirty-five men and women were indicted, including Jack Porter. With a warrant for his arrest, Akron officers went to Porter's residence. When they arrived, he was at home and in the shower. They arrested him, wet and naked. The Escort Case went public, and everyone would be coming to my court.

THE LAWYERS ON THE LIST

Now the Escort Case had arrived on my docket. The first step was to get organized and get the individual defendants on the schedule—a job done by my bailiff, Jill Coleman. Jill was smart, organized, pleasant, discreet and loyal—in short, a terrific bailiff. She had to get each defendant on an appearance schedule to determine if he or she had hired a lawyer or if I would need to appoint one. With so many individuals in one case and so many potential conflicts of interest, I needed many criminal defense lawyers to be sure they had no conflicts.

When I needed to make an appointment, Jill would give me three or four names based on the seriousness of the crime, whether there was an attorney for a co-defendant and the availability of the lawyer. Occasionally, if the defendant was standing in court before me without a lawyer, I would scan the courtroom to find an appropriate attorney who was on hand who could take the case right then. But the Escort Case was unique in many ways. We had to consider the entire list of criminal defense lawyers who were willing and able to handle cases of this magnitude, and we went through them to try to narrow the options. Then Jill started making phone calls to see if each lawyer could accept the appointment or if he or she had a conflict of any kind.

Once we had counsel for each defendant, the job of the lawyer was to meet with the client and start learning about the case. The primary way to get the information was through what is called "discovery." The lawyer literally discovers evidence first from the client and then from the reports, witness statements, documents and physical items the prosecutor has assembled and may use in a trial. The Summit County prosecutor used the "open file" method for discovery. The original file was kept by the prosecutor until needed for trial but available in the prosecutor's office for defense counsel to read but not copy. This was cumbersome at best but broke down completely in the Escort Case.

Lawyers needed to review not only the information relating to their specific client but also the information that related to the case as a whole and how each of the other defendants might relate to their client. The file was voluminous. Dozens of reports of investigation, witness lists, business records, tape recordings and miscellaneous documents filled box after box in the prosecutor's office. Something had to be done to make discovery manageable. Tom Adgate proposed that the defense attorneys organize themselves and share the load. Each attorney was assigned a section of the total file to read through and make notes that would be distributed among all the lawyers. It was tedious but saved time and duplication of effort. Not all the defense lawyers limited their discovery to the group effort. One lawyer made a thorough examination of the documents in the prosecutor's files and then came to see me.

Rob Coombs, a young lawyer, had not practiced law very long before being assigned as counsel for one of the women escorts. A CPA, Rob was bright, conscientious and earnest. He had married the daughter of a judge and had two young children. Several weeks after the Escort Case was filed, I had still conducted no substantive proceedings yet because discovery was ongoing. I was curious when Jill told me that Coombs was in her office asking to see me. He came in and sat down, looking worried. There was no pleasant chit-chat; he said he had something he felt compelled to tell me and did not think I knew. As part of the discovery process, he had been going through the records of the escort services and particularly the lists of their clients. In a stunning moment, he saw the names of four lawyers listed as clients—each of whom now represented one of the defendants in the case.

Coombs wondered if any of the four had already come in to tell me or if any of the other lawyers involved in the case had come forward. They should have seen the same lists. When I told him that no one had told me this, he gave me the names of the four lawyers. Coombs appeared anxious and uncomfortable. I told him that he had done the right thing. However, I said that he was not to tell anyone else and that he had no further obligations. I told him it was my responsibility to address this and that I would. He simply could not understand why no other lawyers had come forward. My thought was that perhaps none of them had been as diligent and thorough as he had been. He left.

This was a mess. In ten years on the bench, nothing close to this had occurred. I don't think I had ever heard or read about such a situation. Because of the rules governing judicial conduct, I couldn't confer with any other judges. I didn't even want my law clerk to know. There was no set path to follow. I looked at the four names—two of these men were in the same law firm.

I called Jill into my chambers. "We have a problem." I told her to contact each of the lawyers and set a time to meet with me individually and to have an assistant prosecutor at the meetings. It didn't have to be Judie Bandy—any assistant prosecutor they sent would be fine. I asked to have Sandy Maxson, the court stenographer assigned to my court, there as well and, if possible, have each of the lawyers come one after the other on the same day. I told her that this was strictly confidential and that even the lawyers were not to know why I wanted to see them. I knew I could rely on her complete discretion and on Sandy's, but I had no faith anyone else would keep quiet.

Sandy Maxson was a highly skilled stenographer who tirelessly recorded every word said in the courtroom whenever we were "on the record." Sandy made that record. Accuracy and speed were of critical importance, and she was both fast and reliable. I trusted Sandy completely. She heard many things that could not be publicly disclosed. I could order that a record of a proceeding be "sealed." The contents were kept confidential, but it would part of the official transcript of the case. Courts and proceedings are public for good reason. Secret tribunals have always been scenes of terrible injustice. But occasionally issues arise that could damage parties or others if publicly disclosed. The risk of private harm can outweigh public importance.

Several days later, the interviews began. The individual lawyers did not know why I wanted to see them. I had a small conference room with a table surrounded by seven chairs. The room had two doors. One door opened from the area where my law clerk worked, and one door opened onto a very short hall that led to my office. The assistant prosecutor, Sandy and I were already in the room when Jill ushered in each lawyer, one at a time.

When there were more than five people in the room, a somewhat claustrophobic feeling developed. I told the lawyer that we were here for a matter related to the Escort Case. I verified that he was representing one or more defendants. Then I said I had learned that in the discovery materials there were lists of clients who had paid for the escorts. I said that on one of the lists was his name. I then waited for a reaction. The first lawyer looked surprised and immediately said, "Well, Judge, that's not me but I will of course recuse myself from this case. I will get off immediately." I told him that was his decision and I would appoint other counsel. He said that would be fine. He stood up and said, "And if there was nothing more?" I said that was all, and he left.

The second lawyer entered and sat down. I went through the same statements and waited for a reaction. This time, there was an indignant denial. "That's not true. That's not me. I never did that." I looked at the assistant prosecutor and said, "It is my understanding that there is no other identifying information such as a credit card number, phone or address linked to this particular name?" The assistant prosecutor replied, "That's correct, Judge." I told the lawyer that he would have to disclose this to his client to determine if a conflict of interest existed and ask if his client wished him to withdraw. He agreed to do that and to advise me. He left.

The third lawyer arrived, and I went through the same litany and waited for his reaction. The lawyer went off like a rocket. "That is outrageous. I never did such a thing. Who is accusing me of this? I never went to a prostitute in my life. How could my name be in those records? Someone is lying." I told him that I was aware of individuals using false names when they went to a brothel or hired a prostitute. I said no one was accusing him. But his name was not common, and it was in the materials seized by the investigating officers. I told him he would have to disclose this to his client and indicate that it may be a conflict of interest. The client would have to decide if she wanted him to continue on the case. He said that nothing like this had ever happened to him before and he was outraged. He said he would discuss it with his client but that he would assure her that it was his name but not him. I told him to advise me whether or not he would remain on the case. He left.

The fourth and last attorney came in and sat down. Once again I recited the circumstances that brought us there and waited for his response. Again there was denial and indignation. "Judge, that's not me. I have a pretty common name so maybe it's someone with my name, but I swear it isn't me. I never went to one of those services. I am no saint, but I didn't hire one of those women." Again I mentioned that it is not uncommon for someone to use a false name under these circumstances. I told him that he had to disclose this to his client and determine if he could still represent her. It was the client's decision to make once she knew the facts. He reassured me that he would and that he would let me know. He left, and I told Sandy to seal the records of the four appearances. I told the assistant prosecutor that if their names were to be included in the evidence in any of the cases that went to trial, I wanted advance notice. I also told him that this matter should be treated as confidential. My confidence in that was not high.

I found the individual reactions of the lawyers interesting. I never accused any of them but had simply stated that each of their names appeared in the escort client records. The two lawyers with strong reactions and denials were in the same law firm. The lawyer who had immediately recused himself denied that he had been a client, but by recusing himself, he almost guaranteed that the matter would go no further. None of the lawyers had seen his own name in the discovery materials. Presumably none had seen the names of the other three lawyers either. Within the following week, two of the three called to say that their clients had no objections and that they would remain on the case. The third lawyer recused himself, and I appointed new counsel for the defendant.

The day after the discussions with the lawyers, Judie Bandy asked if she could see me. Bandy had not been part of the "false names" inquiry but had sent another assistant prosecutor who undoubtedly filled her in. She sat in the chair opposite my desk and perched on the edge as she always did. She never sat back and relaxed. She never leaned against the back or touched the arms of the chair. She sat primly on the edge of the seat as if ready to spring up at any moment. "Judge," she said, "I have to tell you there is another name in the client records. Michael Callahan."

I resisted the urge to slump down in my chair and put my head in my hands. "Oh, lord," I thought. I said, "I guess that is hardly an uncommon name. I suppose if you are going to give a false name, that would really be a whopper. Is that all? Any information other than the name?"

"No."

"Okay. If this is going to come out in evidence at some point, let me know ahead of time."

"I will." With that, she left.

A few months later, I learned that she had not told me everything. That was not, in fact, all.

THE BODY ON THE SIDEWALK

We will never know the death toll resulting from the "War on Drugs." But like with every war, there are casualties. When the Eighteenth Amendment to the U.S. Constitution was adopted in 1919 outlawing the manufacture and sale of alcohol, the unintended consequence was an extensive network of criminals circumventing the law to meet the demands of the drinking public. The same phenomenon happened as we increasingly criminalized drug use and sales. An international network of criminals formed to produce and deliver illegal drugs to an eager public. Those who directly provided the drugs and those who used them were on the front lines and the primary casualties of gun violence and overdoses. Other casualties were not fatalities but rather lives destroyed by incarceration, families crushed, children abandoned and neighborhoods ravaged. One of the uncounted casualties was Melissa Hunt Sublett.

Melissa, also known as "Missy," grew up in a loving home in a stable, working-class area. But early in her teen years, she began using drugs. Her parents, Mattison and Shirley Sublett, struggled to help their daughter. By the age of twenty-nine, she had been arrested nearly thirty times for prostitution and drugs. She was incarcerated in the Marysville State Penitentiary twice. She had occasional periods of sobriety and married Brian D. Hunt. They had three children: Eric, Brandon and Rhiannon. In June 1998, estranged from her husband, she was living with her parents when she told her mother that she was going for a walk. She was wearing jeans and a white tank top. She never came home.

At 5:51 a.m. on June 24, 1998, a call came in to the Akron Police Department reporting someone lying on the sidewalk near 992 5th Avenue and Whitney Street in Akron. Responding officers found Melissa Hunt Sublett dead on that sidewalk, her blood staining the concrete. She had three stab wounds to the heart and seven in the back. Severe contusions revealed that she had been hit on the head and the backs of her legs. The medical examiner estimated that she was murdered some time after 2:00 a.m.

Melissa Hunt Sublett. *Private photo.*

The investigation of Sublett's death began with police canvassing the neighborhood. Had anyone seen or heard anything? Did anyone know Melissa Sublett? What the investigators did not know was that in April, Melissa had called Detective William Ketler of the Copley Police Department, who was assigned to CenTac. She was in the Summit County Jail and told Ketler that she would like to help him out with some drug cases in and around Copley. He went to the jail in April 1998 and talked with her twice. On April 20, 1998, she wrote him a letter:

> *Mr. Bill Ketler, I thought that I would send you a few lines to "thank you" for being my friend and believing in me today. I'm still a little confused about some areas in my life but I know that the Lord is going to walk with me and guide me. I'm really trying to live in the moment Bill, and be proud of the achievements I have made. I'm sending you a special little card that helped me, and I hope that you will hold it close to you too. Thank you for being my friend, and God bless you and your family.*
>
> *Sincerely, Missy.*
>
> *P.S. Thank you for coming and seeing me. I really enjoy talking with you!!!*

Ketler agreed to try to get her released early and contacted her sentencing judge. The judge arranged her release so she could work with Ketler. She got out on June 18. He picked her up at her parents' home in Springfield Township and drove her to Copley. She said that she would show him a few houses on Milan Drive that were drug houses.

When they reached Milan Drive, she pointed out a few different houses, and Ketler said that he already knew that there were drug sales there. He started back toward Springfield, where she lived, and she told him, "I don't trust very many cops."

Ketler replied, "I understand. You've been arrested twenty, thirty times."

She said, "I trust you."

Ketler said, "That's good."

Sublett had good instincts. William "Bill" Ketler was a solid man and a good officer. Of average height and build, he had a shock of thick, slightly unruly, dark hair and a slow, soft smile. Low-key and conscientious, he served on a small police force in a small town. He was married and had a loving family. He was comfortable with his life and his work. Ketler had a fundamental decency that inspired trust. She decided to confide in Bill Ketler.

Sublett said that about two or two and a half years before, in 1996, she was standing at Arlington and Clark Streets in Akron trying to turn a trick. Sometime between 10:30 p.m. and midnight, a black Cadillac pulled to the curb and the window rolled down. A white man sat in the driver's seat. She walked over and told him that she wanted to make some money and party. He said he wanted to party too. She got in the car. He reached into the glove compartment and took out approximately one ounce of powder cocaine. He then said, "You can't say anything to anybody about this. I have a lot to lose." He appeared to be high or drunk. She said it would be forty dollars for a blow job. He then said they were going to the Summit County Courthouse because he was a judge.

Sublett told Ketler that they arrived at the courthouse, and the "judge" parked on the circular driveway between the courthouse and the annex. They

Melissa Hunt Sublett, September 26, 1999. *File photo mug shot.*

walked up the steps to the door on "Front Street," entered and took the elevator. She saw no one else in the courthouse. After leaving the elevator on the third floor, they went to an office and he used a key to get in. Once in the office, he went behind a desk and laid out lines of cocaine, which they inhaled. He turned on some music and asked Melissa to dance. He snorted two more lines of cocaine and lowered his pants down, telling Melissa that he wanted oral sex. He said he didn't have a lot of time. He went into the bathroom to clean up. He returned, and as she was dancing, he seemed to get upset and frustrated. He was trying to use a condom and couldn't get an erection. He then gave her forty dollars and about half a gram of powder cocaine. They went back to his car, and he dropped her off at a house on Edge Street. She knew a lady there named Roberta. She told him that she would see him later, and he drove away. She never saw him again.

When asked by Detective Ketler, Melissa described the office. She remembered chairs and a desk. She saw a short straw in the desk drawer. She then said that there was something else in the office that was unique, maybe a poster or a picture. She did not give a more detailed description. To evaluate the accuracy of Melissa's statement, it is necessary to have an understanding of the layout of the Summit County Courthouse and the annex.

First, the Summit County Courthouse is not on Front Street. The main courthouse is a massive sandstone rectangle that squats on High Street. It has four floors and a basement. Built in 1908, it was once the pride of Summit County. It is designed around a central atrium capped with an ornate skylight. The atrium has walkways encircling it on the second and third floors. The walkways have brass rails guarding the opening and are perfect for leaning and observing. The courtrooms and offices have large doors opening on to the walkways. Over each door there is a sign identifying the courtroom by the name of the judge in large gold letters. There are no courtrooms on the fourth floor.

The main entrance to the courthouse faces High Street and was intended to be quite grand. On the street level two enormous stone lions sit on elevated pedestals, and a wide staircase permits access to the first floor of the building. Before the building was finished, the county commissioners realized that it wasn't going to be large enough. While construction was in progress, a change to the plans was made, and soon a second building, called the annex, was added. It was connected to the main building by a pedestrian bridge that entered the third floor. The public entrance to the annex was on Broadway. A flight of steps led up to the Broadway entrance of the annex from the street level.

A circular driveway ran between the two buildings. On either side of that driveway, under the pedestrian bridge, were two entry doors, one into the annex and one into the basement of the main courthouse. From this driveway, there were no steps leading to either entrance, and neither entrance into the courthouse or the annex is visible from either High Street or Broadway. There were also two entry doors to the main courthouse on High Street. The formal entry at the top of the staircase was seldom used and is now closed. The second entry is located beneath the long formal staircase. It is now also closed. This was the ordinary entrance used by most people and accessed by a walkway from High Street. Neither of these is easily reached from the circular drive. Anyone using the walkway could be seen from High Street, but the entry door itself lies beneath the staircase and could not be seen. Anyone seeking to enter the courthouse or the annex at night who did not wish to be seen could park on the circular drive and enter from the driveway. Entrance through any of the doors at night required a key.

In the main courthouse, the elevator is accessible in the basement. If taken to the third floor, it opens onto the walkway that surrounds the atrium. The courtroom assigned to Judge Michael Callahan was on the third floor and could be entered from the atrium walkway. Every courtroom has a private office for the judge with a private bathroom. The elevator starts in the basement. If it's taken to the second floor, someone unfamiliar with the building could assume they were at the third level of the building and therefore on the third floor.

Melissa Sublett told Detective Ketler that she went up steps to enter the courthouse. This would be consistent with entering the annex from Broadway. The Domestic Relations courtrooms and magistrates' offices were on the second floor of the annex. She said that the "judge's" car was parked on the circular drive. This would enable them to enter unobserved into the courthouse basement, but they would not go up steps to do so. She was not familiar with the buildings. She thought that the courthouse was on Front Street. Once inside the building, she said they took the elevator to the third floor and that the "judge" used a key to unlock his office. Judge Callahan's office and courtroom were on the third floor.

The day after Melissa's disclosure, Ketler picked her up at her parents' home and took her downtown to the Summit County Courthouse. He asked if she could remember where she had been on that night. They went into the courthouse and up to the third floor, and he let her look around without him physically next to her. She walked over to Judge Callahan's chambers. Ketler joined her in the walkway as she looked into the open doorway. They did not go into the chambers, but Melissa looked in far enough to say, "That's the one. I remember the office." She said there was something distinguishable about the office, but she wasn't sure what. In June 1998, in Judge Callahan's office, there was a life-size standee of movie actor John Wayne. It had been a recent birthday gift. But it was not in the office in 1996 when Melissa went to the courthouse

Judge Michael Callahan and sidekick John Wayne. *From the* Akron Beacon Journal.

that night. However, if she saw the poster when she looked into the office with Ketler, she did not identify it as what she remembered.

Ketler then asked her if she could identify the car, and she said maybe she could. The detective took her down to the circular driveway. Several cars were parked there. The detective said, "Just look around, see if you see anything that looks familiar." She walked around and saw a dark Cadillac. She came over to Ketler, visibly shaking and disturbed. She said, "That's it. I remember the baseball hats in the back window." That Cadillac belonged to Judge Michael Callahan.

Ketler told Melissa to keep all this a secret. She said she had never before told anyone. While he did not show her a photograph of Michael Callahan, later Ketler was asked if she gave him a physical description of the person she claims picked her up in the Cadillac. Ketler said, "The physical matches pretty much"—referring to Callahan. In a subsequent interview, Ketler said that she described a big man, rather tall, with brown hair, but she didn't mention a beard.

When Melissa first talked with Ketler, she not only discussed her visit to the courthouse but also told him about relationships with two other men, a Summit County deputy who worked at the jail and an Akron police officer who at that time worked in the Identification Bureau. She said that when she lived on Heddon Avenue in Akron as a teenager, this officer patrolled the neighborhood. He was part of a police "ride along" program to promote community relations, and at some point, she signed a waiver to ride with him. They became good friends. Frequently she would ride with him, and eventually they had sex. Later, when she got older and worked as a prostitute on Arlington and Clark Streets, he would pick her up in his cruiser, take her to a "crack house" and drop her off. She would buy crack cocaine and meet him nearby. She smoked it in the cruiser, and they would have sex. He also took her to an address on Wellington Avenue in East Akron to buy crack and drove her around in the cruiser as she smoked it. He never used the drugs.

Melissa also disclosed a sexual relationship with the Summit County deputy who may have been the father of one of her children. Ketler reported everything to his CenTac supervisors, Summit County deputy Larry Limbert and Akron police captain Craig Gilbride, as well as Judie Bandy. Six days later, on June 24, the Akron Police Department opened an investigation into the murder of Melissa Hunt Sublett, but the investigating officers knew nothing about Melissa's disclosures to Ketler. Their investigation did not include her trip to the courthouse. If the officers had known, they might have discovered another "judge" who could have taken her into the courthouse that night and who might have wanted her dead.

The Summit County Domestic Relations Court was located on the second floor of the annex. It housed the two full-time judges and several magistrates. In many ways, magistrates function as judges. They conduct hearings, issue rulings and manage cases. A magistrate's decision is not final until approved and signed by an elected judge. They appear in robes and are addressed as "Your Honor." To the average person, a magistrate is a judge. When Melissa Sublett went with a "judge" into the courthouse that night, Magistrate C. Don Morris was an employee in the Domestic Relations Court. His office was on the second floor. Morris had a key to the building and from time to time came into the annex to work on weekends. He would occasionally ask one of his fellow magistrates if she might be coming in to work on the weekend. She thought that was odd. Why would he want to know that?

Morris used cocaine, and his drug addiction grew more serious over time, interfering with his work. Domestic Relations judge Judy Nicely was concerned. She counseled Morris about his work and his drug use, which he didn't deny. Then he was arrested in 1995. Police on patrol observed a black Cadillac stop to pick up a prostitute on Arlington Street in Akron. One year later, Melissa Sublett was picked up in a dark Cadillac on Arlington Street.

During his arrest, the officers found drugs in the vehicle and charged him with drug possession. Morris's case was referred to Judge Elinore Marsh Stormer in Akron Municipal Court.

Judge Stormer pioneered drug courts to treat addiction and stop the continued cycle of addicts revolving through the criminal justice system. She recognized that Morris had a serious addiction, one that was going to destroy his career and perhaps his life. She ordered him into non-residential treatment at Oriana House, a treatment facility for alcohol and drug addiction. While in treatment, he continued his work at the court. Morris completed the program, but relapse is an expected part of recovery, as individuals struggle with the physical craving for the drug and the psychological need.

Judge Judy Nicely and her fellow Domestic Relations judge Carol Deszo received a request to meet with County Sheriff Richard Warren. He told them that two deputy sheriffs who provided security for the courthouse had seen someone come into the courthouse at night accompanied by a woman. They suspected that this person—who drove a black Cadillac— was using the courthouse for illicit sex. They had two suspects: Magistrate Morris and William Diehl. William "Bill" Diehl worked security in Domestic Relations Court. A Summit County special deputy, Bill was well-liked and personable. He was middle-aged, average-looking and would never be described as a "hunk." The judges found it unlikely that Diehl was involved. When interviewed, both men denied the allegations. Despite identifying a black Cadillac, no license plate number was recorded by the deputies. This oversight is hard to comprehend. The investigation went no further, and the judges decided that they had insufficient evidence to reach any conclusions.

Morris continued working and continued using drugs. His work got further behind. Judge Nicely tried to help him, setting deadlines for his work, but when he did not improve, she fired him. His life continued a downward spiral. When he was arrested in April 2001, he had a non-reducible felony drug charge. Judge Mary Spicer served as the Felony Drug Court judge. Like her predecessor, she tried to work with Morris and placed him in treatment again. For a while, he seemed to improve and completed his probationary treatment period, until once again the need for the drugs took over.

Arrested again in April 2002, he risked prison and hired one of the top criminal defense lawyers in Summit County, Kerry O'Brien. Once again Morris went before Judge Spicer. He and his lawyer needed to persuade the judge that this time he would actually beat his addiction. Morris pleaded no contest to permitting drug abuse in a motor vehicle. The judge found him guilty and ordered him to serve thirty days in the Summit County

Jail with three years' probation and further drug treatment. Perhaps something clicked because his probation terminated on April 14, 2005, and Morris had no further drug charges in Summit County. He lost his license to practice law.

William R. Diehl was well-liked and personable. He was a friendly man who talked and joked with everyone who came past his desk. He provided security for the Domestic Relations Court, where emotions often ran high and conflict was almost inevitable. Before the Summit County sheriff had reported to the judges that a man was seen bringing a woman into the courthouse, William Diehl had asked to talk with Judge Deszo. He came into her office with a worried look and said that an unusual thing had happened. While he was working at his desk in the annex, a young woman had approached him and begun talking. She propositioned him. Diehl was wearing his deputy's uniform. Diehl declined her offer and laughed it off. Then, when he was working a few days later, it happened again—the same woman came into the courthouse and offered him sex. Again, he said no. Diehl told Judge Deszo that this was disturbing to him and that he was puzzled. The judge thought this was extremely odd. Why would a woman proposition a sheriff's deputy in uniform in the courthouse? She told "Mr. Bill," as she called him, that she was glad he told her and to let her know if it happened again. Later, when the sheriff told the judges that deputies had seen a man bring a woman into the courthouse annex at night, both judges found it unlikely that Bill Diehl was the man. But how well do you know the people you work with?

On May 1, 2000, Copley Police set up a sting for "Johns" who were picking up prostitutes in Copley. They used a confidential informant, Aimee L. Peterjohn, who was wearing a wire transmitter. A motel room nearby was also wired. This is where she was to take the "John" who picked her up. The man who picked up Peterjohn was William R. Diehl. He was charged with soliciting, a third-degree misdemeanor. He was not arrested. He was given a summons to appear. When he came to the police station, he was questioned by Detective William Ketler of Copley. Diehl was cocky and defiant. He told Ketler that he was a Summit County special deputy sheriff and implied that all this this would be taken care of. On August 27, 2000, he pleaded guilty in Barberton Municipal Court, and Diehl only paid court costs of fifty dollars.

Diehl had been told by his attorney that if he pleaded guilty, that would end it and no one would know. But keeping that sort of thing secret is impossible. It was soon common knowledge, and the newspaper picked it up. Diehl went to the domestic relations judges and apologized profusely.

He said that the woman in Copley whom he picked up that night was the same woman who had propositioned him in the courthouse. He had been planning to go out that evening and play cards, but he got a call from the woman. This time, he took the bait. She told him where to meet her, and he drove to the Copley motel, where he was arrested. He was mortified by what he had done. His wife was also publicly humiliated. This looked like a setup.

The two judges were angry with Diehl, but they believed that he had been set up. They asked for a meeting with Sheriff Richard Warren, who promptly agreed to see them. They laid out the events as recounted by Diehl and stated that both thought he had been set up. Judge Deszo was angry because the woman had been sent to proposition him in the court reception area with families and children present. Judge Nicely thought that he had been entrapped. Sheriff Warren admitted that it had been a setup by his deputies. The judges demanded an investigation. They both thought that C. Don Morris was the man seen going into the courthouse with a woman.

Sheriff Warren did not seem particularly concerned with what they said. Weeks went by with no word from the sheriff and no investigation. Judges Nicely and Deszo decided not to fire Diehl because although he had succumbed to temptation, they knew he had been set up—the sheriff told them. But they did not know why.

It was known that Bill Diehl drove a black Cadillac. As a security officer, he undoubtedly had a key to the courthouse annex. He was five-foot-ten, about two hundred pounds and had brown hair. He would be the perfect man to point to as a suspect. If there was a coverup, creating another suspect was a classic diversion. When Ketler first interviewed William Diehl, Ketler did not know that a man was seen by the sheriff's deputies taking a woman into the courthouse. He had no reason to connect William Diehl with Melissa Sublett. Ketler was interviewing Diehl as just another "John" looking for sex in Copley. He did not know that Aimee Peterjohn had called Diehl and told him to come to the motel in Copley. Was Diehl the man in the black Cadillac who picked up Melissa Sublett and took her to the courthouse that night? Perhaps. It was more likely that Diehl was being set up as a suspect to divert suspicion from someone else.

Three men drove dark Cadillacs and had keys to the Summit County Courthouse. Two of them, Morris and Diehl, were arrested for picking up prostitutes on the street. Two of them, Callahan and Morris, were "judges." Callahan was identified by Melissa Sublett as the man who picked her up that night to party and whose office she remembered along with baseball caps in the back of his Cadillac. Morris was known to use drugs and was addicted to cocaine. Morris and Diehl were clean-shaven. Of the three, Callahan matched the physical description given by Sublett—except he had a beard and Melissa never mentioned a beard in describing the man she said was Callahan.

Of course, it is not necessary to conclude that any one of these men came into the courthouse at night accompanied by a woman. It is also possible that one or two or all three could have at one time or another taken different women into the courthouse or the annex. Any of them could have parked his dark Cadillac in the circular drive and used a personal key for entry. All three of these men would "have a lot to lose" if caught in the act or if it was disclosed by someone. So who was it?

WHO KILLED MELISSA SUBLETT?

Several driving forces steered the Escort Case on its tortured path. One factor was the personalities of key participants. A second arose from the political ambitions of the men and women involved. Michael Callahan became the appointed Summit County prosecutor in January 1999 when Maureen O'Connor became lieutenant governor of Ohio. This required him to run in the general election in November 2000. He also had to run in the Republican primary.

But that was still to come in the spring of 1999. The next months were quiet as defense attorneys worked through discovery, filing multiple defense motions while I tried to facilitate the process to the extent I could. In March, Tom Adgate organized a system for cooperative discovery, with each defense attorney taking notes on part of the total file and then sharing them among all the lawyers by copying them. As each worked through the process, they discussed the options with their clients. I knew that once the first plea bargains began, the process would start moving.

Laura Ridenour was the first major target to plead guilty. Ridenour's lawyer, Tom Ciccolini, was smart, experienced and very good at seeing where his client's best interests lay. He had good "client control," as they say in the profession. When a defendant decides to accept a plea bargain, often a prosecutor may want a "proffer" as a condition. The pleading defendant makes a sworn statement of evidence that the prosecutor can use to convince other defendants to plead guilty or to use if the pleading defendant testifies against a co-defendant. This statement is called a proffer.

Top: Laura Ridenour arrested by Akron Police, January 9, 2000. *Paul Tople, Akron Beacon Journal.*

Bottom: Laura Ridenour. *File photo mug shot.*

Ridenour and Ciccolini met with Judie Bandy, and Ridenour gave a long proffer. She revealed several things that the prosecution did not know about Porter, Fulkerson, Moats, the clients of the service and the various women who worked for Touch of Class.

As individual escort cases worked toward resolution, something else was also going on. In December 1998, Stephanie Williams had been arrested by the Akron police for the murder of Melissa Sublett. After a six-month investigation, they had amassed enough evidence to indict Williams for aggravated murder, a special felony. Stephanie Williams knew Melissa; they used drugs together. Both served time in prison and knew many of the same people. Williams's mother, Hattie Williams, was a prostitute and drug user who lived with her mother, Queenie Brazil, at 602 Winans Avenue, the house where the police concluded Melissa died. Within a week of the murder, investigators had identified Hattie's daughter Stephanie as someone potentially involved and questioned her at police headquarters.

Later after her arrest, Williams was arraigned in Akron Municipal Court before Judge Brenda Burnham Unruh, who appointed a defense lawyer for her, Tom Adgate. Adgate began investigating the circumstances around Sublett's death. The case went to Judge James E. Murphy in Common Pleas Court. Judge Murphy chose a second lawyer for Williams, Don Malarcik, young and inexperienced, to start working with Adgate.

A gregarious, sarcastic Irishman who loved all things Notre Dame, Judge James Murphy was well-liked by the law enforcement community and plugged into the rumor mill in the courthouse. He enjoyed the camaraderie of the lawyers who practiced in his court and was something of a "wisecracker," often humorous but too often at someone else's expense.

A motion filed by defense counsel in the Williams prosecution revealed that at the time of her death, Melissa Sublett was working undercover with Detective Ketler for CenTac. This got the judge's attention. He ordered Melissa's handler, Ketler, to produce records for inspection by the court. Then Tom Adgate called the judge and said that Detective Russ McFarland of the Akron police had attempted to get his client to sign a waiver to move to an out-of-state prison for her protection, which was highly unusual. The judge called Assistant Prosecutor Scott Reilly and Detective McFarland to meet with him. They arrived at Judge Murphy's chambers with McFarland's supervisor, Sergeant Harold Craig.

The judge asked what was going on. McFarland said that he was trying to get Williams sent from Marysville Penitentiary to another penitentiary for her own safety. She was in danger from other inmates in Marysville. While awaiting trial in Akron for the Sublett murder, Williams had been sentenced on another case and sent to Marysville. Then she was transferred to a prison in New Jersey. Judge Murphy wanted her held in Marysville until the trial. As the men were leaving, McFarland said, "Judge, I got to talk to you one to one with nobody present." The judge said, "Russ, that's what gets us into these kinds of jackpots. I will not allow it."

That's how matters stood on Monday, April 5, 1999. A meeting was held in the judge's chambers with his court reporter, Margaret Wellemeyer, present to make a record of what was said. Detective Ketler, Assistant Prosecutors Scott Reilly and Jonathan Menuez and defense attorneys Tom Adgate and Don Malarcik were all present. Judge Murphy began by telling them that some of these things were very sensitive and that he wanted them kept in that room. The record of proceedings was to be sealed and not unsealed or transcribed until he ordered it.

Ketler provided the judge with the four pages of handwritten notes he took when he talked with Melissa Sublett on June 18—six days before her murder. Ketler had not prepared a full report of investigation, an ROI, for CenTac's files. He prepared a partial report only relating to "Judge Callahan," which was in the CenTac files. Ketler revealed Melissa's account of her nighttime trip to the courthouse and their own recent visit when she identified the third-floor office and the black Cadillac with the baseball caps. He also related her sexual relationships with the Akron police officer and the deputy sheriff. The defense lawyers and the prosecutors asked questions of

Ketler. The court reporter marked Ketler's notes as an exhibit as part of the sealed record, but although the transcript was subsequently unsealed and made public, the handwritten notes were not released. The notes were kept by the court reporter until 2007, when they were destroyed as part of the routine purging of closed case records.

Judge Murphy persisted in trying to determine why McFarland wanted to talk with him privately. Scott Reilly stated that he knew McFarland and others had been interviewing women in Marysville about Williams. Reilly concluded that Williams wasn't in jeopardy—it was the women who were going to testify against her who were in danger. These imprisoned women contacted the detectives to ask for protection. That's why Williams was sent to New Jersey by the state authorities at the prison.

During Williams's time in Marysville before and after her indictment for the Sublett murder, other versions of her story emerged. Ketler and Sergeant Larry White learned that a woman, Witness X, was presently in the Summit County Jail and had knowledge about the Melissa Sublett murder. On December 17, 1998, they went to the jail to interview her.

Witness X told Ketler and White that she had known Missy (Melissa Sublett) "very well" for about fifteen years. She said that although she knew Missy was a prostitute and heavily into drugs, Missy was not into ripping off "Johns" to support her habit. The last time she actually saw Missy was in Marysville. She got out before Missy and did not know that Missy was released until she heard that she was killed. Witness X said that on the night of June 23 and the early morning of June 24, she was working at the corner of Baird and Talbot, a location that Missy was known to frequent. But she did not see Missy at all that night.

She also said she had known Stephanie Williams for five years. She said Stephanie did not have much to do with men; however, she would associate with them whenever she wanted drugs. She and Stephanie had an amicable relationship and remained friends. The two women were together for a half an hour on the day Missy was killed. Witness X was at a drug house when Stephanie arrived in a car driven by an unknown male. Stephanie was desperate for some crack and asked if a specific individual had some. Witness X told Stephanie that he was sleeping and that she wasn't going to wake him. Stephanie talked Witness X into leaving with her to buy crack. They got into the car. Witness X could not identify the driver. He kept his face forward, so she never got a good look at him.

They drove to a location looking for a dealer whom Stephanie thought could sell her some dope. Witness X said that Stephanie was very "noided" (street slang for hyper), and it was obvious that Stephanie was already high and used drugs earlier. Witness X soon regretted going on this trip. A short time later, they met a known east side dealer sitting in a black Monte Carlo in a parking lot. Witness X bought some crack but refused to share with Stephanie, who was looking for a handout or getting it "on credit" and probably didn't have the money to make a buy. The two women parted company.

It wasn't until the next day that Witness X saw Stephanie Williams again. She went to the apartment where Stephanie was staying. Several people were there using drugs. She said Stephanie and her friend Crissy were in their bedroom off by themselves. There she learned about Missy's murder.

Ketler asked, "Do you know who killed Missy?"

She replied, "Stephanie Williams and someone else."

Ketler asked, "Why?"

"When I first talked to her in jail [August 1998], Stephanie told me she didn't have anything to do with it. But later before Stephanie left for Marysville [Ohio Reformatory for Women] she told me, 'I didn't kill Missy. I just hit her in the head with a baseball bat.' Witness X said that Stephanie is under the impression that the cause of Missy's death was the stabbing and thus downplays her involvement by using the baseball bat."

Ketler asked, "Do you know if Stephanie had access to a baseball bat?"

"She kept two baseball bats there [in the apartment] at the top of the steps just inside the kitchen. One was silver—like that pipe [pointing to aluminum conduit in the interview room]. One of the bats was aluminum and one had a taped handle."

"Who did she think the other assailant could be?"

"I believe Von [Hattie Williams, Stephanie Williams's mother] and _____ had something to do with it. I don't think _____ had anything to do with it but she knows who did. _____ is afraid of Stephanie. Even the deputies know that. Stephanie is scandalous, a bully, an intimidator."

"Where did the murder take place?"

"I heard it happened inside 998 Baird and her body was taken to 5th and dumped. _____ knows Queenie Brazil [Stephanie's grandmother] and said that another woman deals crack out of Queenie's house but never heard that Missy was possibly killed there."

"Is Stephanie sorry that she was involved in Missy's death?"

"Stephanie has no remorse. She's not sorry Missy is dead. She just wants the police to leave her alone."

The officers thanked Witness X for her time and she said that she would testify if needed. She said, "They didn't need to kill that girl. She'd never harm anybody."

Ketler attended the autopsy of Melissa Sublett and subsequently talked with Dr. Marvin Platt, who performed it. Dr. Platt said that a massive skull fracture caused by a baseball bat, pipe or similar blunt-force object was used as the means of causing the death. The stab wounds were inflicted as the victim was dying and hastened the death. The blood evidence established that the killing did not occur on the sidewalk where the body was found. She had been killed elsewhere, and then her body was brought to the sidewalk.

Putting a knife into another person is a grisly process. It takes strength and determination. Melissa was stabbed ten different times. Someone kept putting the knife in her body over and over. She was both stabbed ten times and severely beaten in the head. Why? An argument over drugs doesn't rise to the level of frenzy that results in a death this brutal. Motive for a criminal act is important. It often explains facts that otherwise make little sense. If, as Williams implied, others thought that Melissa was a snitch, working with the police and wearing a wire, this would establish a motive to silence her. But that would not explain the brutality that was used. If it was a drug issue, a drive-by shooting at night as she stood on the street would be easy, and a quick getaway would leave little evidence for the police to find.

Additional versions of the murder began to surface. On December 28, 1998, two phone calls were made. The first came from the mother of a woman who was incarcerated at Marysville Penitentiary. This call went to Detective Jenifer Limbert, a Summit County deputy sheriff. The caller stated that her daughter had heard Stephanie Williams bragging about the murder of Melissa Sublett. According to the caller, Williams said that she killed Sublett by hitting her in the head with a baseball bat. The caller's daughter, Witness #1, said this statement was made prior to Williams being taken back to Summit County for arraignment on the aggravated murder. Deputy Limbert called Detective McFarland and told him what the woman had said.

The second call came from Witness #2. She told Sergeant Larry White of the Akron police that she and another inmate, Witness #3, heard Stephanie Williams talking about her involvement in Sublett's murder. Sergeant White relayed this information to McFarland. McFarland arranged to go to Marysville and interview the three witnesses. The three women were interviewed separately, and the interviews were taped.

Witness #1 gave her statement on January 2, 1999. She said, "Last Wednesday, December 23, Stephanie Williams came to my table and sat with me and another inmate. She started talking about Melissa Sublett. I knew Melissa Sublett from when she and I were down here [at Marysville] in 1994. When I first came down here this time, in June, I had found out that Missy was murdered, through other inmates that had come in through Summit County, but I never heard any details, until Stephanie started talking."

The witness continued, "Stephanie was bragging last week that she hid a baseball bat and a knife. She said there was a guy called '747' in the house down in the basement. Stephanie kept watching from a window. She kept watching while Missy was down in the basement with him. I believe the guy's first name was _____ or _____, something on that order. Like I said she mentioned a baseball bat and a knife that they were found [by the police]. It really blew my mind for her to bring this up and I didn't know anything about it before she started talking."

McFarland asked Witness #1 if Stephanie knew whether "747" knew Missy? She said no. He then asked if Stephanie ever gave a reason for the killing.

She said, "Uh, yeah. At the time she was murdered they thought Missy was wired. There was mention of her wearing shorts and a halter top. They thought that Missy was snitching on them."

McFarland asked if Stephanie Williams ever mentioned to her that Stephanie was injured during the incident.

Witness #1 replied, "Stephanie never mentioned getting hurt. She kept talking about walking to the window, opening the curtains and watching for the police."

McFarland said, "From what you're saying, Stephanie Williams is saying that '747' did all of it."

Witness #1 answered, "Yes."

He asked, "She didn't say to you that she used the baseball bat?"

"No. She said that she hid one."

"And we [the police] found the baseball bat?"

"Right. Right. The police also found the knife in a purse." Witness #1 did not know if it was Stephanie's purse or Missy's purse.

McFarland's next question was if Stephanie had mentioned any others involved, especially women.

Witness #1 responded, "She said there was someone else there. Stephanie kept referring to 'they.' The name '747' kept coming up."

"Were any of her relatives there?"

"No, I didn't hear that part."

"Did Stephanie mention if this happened inside or outside?"

"It sounded like inside because she kept talking about going to a window and looking out to see if the police were coming."

"Did Stephanie ever tell you how Missy got from the place where she was killed to the outdoor place where her body was found?"

"No, she didn't."

"Did Stephanie ever mention handling the body at all?"

"I didn't hear her say that. No."

McFarland mentioned two names and asked if either one was familiar. She said one was, but she couldn't remember why. He asked, "Did Stephanie tell you what street the murder took place in?"

"No."

"Did Stephanie tell you she had talked to the police?"

"No. She just said that Summit County was on the way to Marysville to pick her up."

McFarland next inquired about Stephanie's attitude. "How did she feel about the incident? Was she worried about it or not?"

"Hell no. Hell no. She thinks it's all joke and that's what upsets me the most."

"What's a joke? The death itself or the case the police have against her?"

"The death itself. It was more than just table talk. There was no conscience. No remorse. She's arrogant and has no feeling."

"Did Stephanie ever say how long she had known Missy?"

"No."

"When they had time to find out that Missy wasn't wired after they killed her, did they say anything about that? Like they were wrong about it?"

"No."

Witness #2 was the next interview McFarland conducted. He asked the woman to tell him what she had to say.

She began, "It was a couple of days….She [Stephanie] was in the bed and she was crying. She was really out of control. Some girl came up to me and said, 'You need to go….' She [Stephanie] told me that she had to tell me something. So I took her into the bathroom into the back stall. And that's when she told me that she killed this girl named Missy."

The witness continued, "This is what she said happened. Stephanie said that they were getting high and Missy had a lot of dope and money. And she was threatening to leave and they did not want her to leave. So when she tried to leave…_____ tried to stop her from leaving. So they got into a tussle. Stephanie picked up a baseball bat and hit Missy in the head a couple of times and stabbed her and this guy named '747' took the body and threw it on 5ᵗʰ Avenue….So I went and got _____ and I brought her back and I made Stephanie repeat what she said to me in front of _____. I walked away and let them talk for a minute. I was done and the real reason I got _____ is because I couldn't believe Stephanie was telling me all this. She [Stephanie] had so many different stories. I got _____ knowing Stephanie would tell _____ the truth."

McFarland asked, "Since Stephanie had so many different stories, did you believe Stephanie was being truthful with her?"

Witness #2 replied, "That's what she said. She never told me the other stories. She had been telling other people other stories. That's what the others had been saying. What she told me is what I told you. And she also told this story to _____. _____ knows more. She knows what Stephanie did with the weapon 'cause she caught the whole story. I didn't want the whole story because I got scared. They [the police] will get you for Complicity if you don't tell them when someone tells you something like this."

McFarland reassured Witness #2 by telling her that she didn't have anything to worry about since she was giving a voluntary statement. "I told her that she did not have to prove the things that Stephanie said were true. We were very appreciative that she was coming forward and she was doing the right thing."

Then McFarland asked her a series of questions, starting with, "Did she [Stephanie] ever state she ever got hurt, in any way, during the incident?"

"You would have to talk to _____ about that because Stephanie really went into detail with her."

"Did she give the location of where this [murder] took place?"

"She told that to _____."

"Did she [Stephanie] tell you if it happened inside or outside?"

"She said it started inside and happened outside."

"And '747' transported the body to where the body was found?"

"Yeah, but I don't know who '747' is."

"Do you know where he is at now?"

"No."

"Do you know if he [747] has been involved in anything else?"

"I thought she said he was in jail."

"She didn't tell you what for?"

Witness #2 shook her head no and said, "Huh-uh. She just said he was in jail."

"How close are you to Stephanie?"

"Real close."

"Could you testify against Stephanie if subpoenaed?"

"Yes."

"Did I make you any promises?"

"No sir."

"Did I make any threats?"

"No sir."

"Is this a strictly voluntary statement you've given me?"

"Yes sir."

"Did you take the initiative on your own to get information to the Akron Police Department?"

"Yes."

"What did you do?"

"I called this number [375-2490] and I talked to this lady [Detective Baker] and she hooked me up to Sergeant White."

"Did you talk to Mr. Hoffman before you made this call? [Hoffman was an employee at the penitentiary.]"

"Yes, I did."

McFarland thanked her for her statement and for her initiative, and that concluded the interview.

Witness #3 was interviewed, but no transcription of that statement was filed in the records of the case.

The next step in the investigation by McFarland was another trip to Marysville Penitentiary on February 21, 1999. He was accompanied by Sergeant Sean Matheny. This trip was to interview Witness #4. McFarland noted, "Witness #4 _____ is not a violent person and felt compelled to come forward with what she learned and do the right thing by telling the police. She made a voluntary tape recorded statement without promise of benefit."

Witness #4 said that she met Stephanie Williams in Marysville. In time, Stephanie opened up and told her that she was under indictment for aggravated murder. Stephanie told Witness #4 initially that she had done it. But that changed as time went on. Witness #4 said that she never paid much attention to what Stephanie was saying at first. She said that Stephanie got to talking about this Missy being a crack smoker and Stephanie's mom being a prostitute. Stephanie complained about growing up in a home like that. Witness #4 had a lot of compassion for her at this point and said, "You could tell she had a really messed up childhood."

Further into the conversation, it appeared that Stephanie really trusted Witness #4. Stephanie started talking openly about her mom and their drug use. Witness #4 said she told Stephanie about the different drug rehab programs available to her at Marysville. Then, late one night, Witness #4 was sitting on a lock box watching television. Stephanie joined her and told her that Stephanie did commit the murder. Stephanie told her that there were two men involved. Witness #4 didn't know for sure the names of the men involved. Stephanie started to go into detail about what happened that night.

Stephanie said that Missy had been coming to her house all day, buying crack and smoking it. Stephanie said that Missy was a prostitute. She said, "I guess they are out of money and were running out of crack. Some guy went and got Missy and brought her back to Stephanie's apartment. It wasn't at her grandmother's. She didn't tell me where her apartment was. When he brought Missy back to the apartment, Stephanie said she wanted some money from Missy but there wasn't any more crack."

Witness #4 continued, "A fight broke out and she [Stephanie] hit Missy with a bat. They took her out and put her, I think, in _____'s car. I don't know why that name keeps sticking in my mind. They took her out to a vacant lot and Stephanie said she stabbed her three times in the back and twice in the front. Then Stephanie said while Missy was lying on the ground, she was moaning and obviously not dead. So Stephanie then struck her again in the head." As Stephanie told Witness #4 this, she demonstrated for her with arm movements and standing in such a way as to be striking someone on the ground.

Witness #4 continued, "Stephanie said it crushed the whole side of her face. They took her body [somewhere] and then she told me that when she got back to her place she noticed that she [Stephanie] had been cut underneath her rib cage. She pulled up her shirt and I saw that she had a scar."

McFarland noted that as Witness #4 was telling this, she pointed to a spot on her side under her left arm indicating where on Stephanie the scar appeared. Witness #4 went on and said, "Stephanie had told her that Missy's purse was still in her apartment when she got back to it. Stephanie took the purse and the ball bat and hid them in the basement. Stephanie told Witness #4 that she knew this would be evidence against her. For a short time, Stephanie forgot about the bat and the purse."

Now the interview shifted to questions from McFarland and answers by Witness #4. McFarland asked if Stephanie had mentioned what happened to the knife.

She said, "Stephanie did not."

Sergeant Matheny asked, "Who stabbed Missy?"

She replied, "I am pretty sure she said that she stabbed Missy but I can't be positive. It was late at night and I was getting frightened by the story. I know for a fact that she told me she hit Missy with the ball bat."

Matheny then asked, "And she told you that she did it twice? Once at the house and once, apparently harder, at the scene of the murder?"

"Yeah. Yes. Yes, sir."

McFarland asked, "Was there any mention of where Missy was killed as being a separate location from where her body was found?"

"No. They said that when [pause]…well, yes there was. They had put Missy in the trunk of this _____ guy's car and taken her out of the lot. They then took her somewhere else to take her out of the trunk. I don't know if _____ is the right name I heard."

McFarland asked, "Was there a mention of any nicknames?"

"I don't know if _____ is the right name. I know that _____ is the name that sticks in my head."

Matheny said, "You reported this to Ms. Anunike two days before Christmas?"

"Yes."

"And she immediately typed up the information you reported to her?"

"Yeah."

"She typed on here that you said the name was 'Robert.'"

McFarland noted her face immediately lit up and she said, "That's the name. Robert. And there was another one. There were two people."

Matheny asked, "But the name Robert is definitely the name of the main male involved? Because that's the name you gave Ms. Anunike when it was fresh in your mind?"

"Yes. There were two men that day. One of them brought Missy to that house and he's not the same person who had the car."

McFarland asked, "Did Stephanie mention any women being involved?"

"No."

"Any relatives?"

"No, just her and the two men. The one that brought Missy and the one that Stephanie left the house with [with Missy's body]."

"What happened to the purse in the basement?"

"Stephanie did not not tell me that. She did not tell me what happened to the baseball bat."

Several names were mentioned to Witness #4, but she said that there was no mention of any of them. In reference to another name, Witness #4 said, "Stephanie did mention _____. I think that was in conjunction with her mother and her mother was a prostitute."

McFarland asked, "Did she ever mention a Kerri?"

"Yes. She did mention a Kerri. Kerri is the one she told about the purse and everything. Stephanie said Kerri was supposed to be taking care of business while Stephanie was here. I don't know what 'taking care of business' meant." McFarland had previously interviewed Kerri Heiser. Heiser had told him that she had taken Stephanie to the hospital. Heiser had also put money into Stephanie's inmate account at the Summit County Jail after Stephanie was indicted.

McFarland asked, "Did Stephanie ever mention going to the hospital for that cut?"

"No. She never mentioned going to the hospital. She just lifted up her top. It was pink colored and fresh. I asked her how she got through County without them searching her and finding the wound. She told them at County that it was a glass cut. You can look at it and tell it ain't no glass cut."

"Did she ever mention talking to the police before her arrest?"

"Nope."

"Since her arrest?"

"Yes. She said the police came to her once. She never told me about the conversation that they had. At first, initially when she told me about the indictment, she told me she didn't do it. Later she told me she had done it and whatever she had done and everything. She asked how I thought she should pursue the case. I just told her, 'I don't know.'"

"Had Stephanie ever told her where Robert was or _____ was at now?"

"No."

McFarland asked, "Was Stephanie afraid of them?"

"No. She never acted like she was afraid of them. I took it as though those were her buddies, the way she talked about them."

"Did she ever display any remorse or sorrow over what happened?"

"She just said that Missy was a 'crack ho.' Basically that's how she referred to her the whole time. Less than human because she was a 'crack ho.' That was something that really disturbed me."

"Have you discussed this with any other inmates?"

"No."

"Did any other inmates approach you about this?"

"No."

Witness #4 told the officers that she had discussed this with her psychologist and two other staff people. Originally, she went to a prison official because she was afraid of Stephanie, and subsequently she was called to the office of the investigator for the Department of Corrections. He suggested she tell the

Akron detectives what she knew about Stephanie's statements. She agreed to do so because she knew it was the right thing to do. She told the officers she had no problem testifying. She voluntarily submitted to a polygraph examination and passed as being truthful on all questions asked.

Williams was transported back from New Jersey to Summit County and held in the county jail. She met with her lawyers to discuss a plea offer made by the prosecution. On June 9, 1999, with attorneys Adgate and Malarcik present, Williams entered a guilty plea to a reduced charge of involuntary manslaughter, felony of the third degree. She received an agreed sentence of three years' incarceration with credit for time served, resulting in additional incarceration of slightly over two years. This was a drastic reduction in the sentence she faced for aggravated murder. It was later characterized as the "deal of the century." As part of the plea deal, Williams made a proffer to Assistant Summit County Prosecutor Scott Reilly, Detective Russ McFarland of Akron and Sergeant Larry White.

Over the course of six months, Stephanie Williams gave several different versions of what happened on the night of Sublett's murder. At the time of her proffer, Robert L. Thomas was an inmate in Belmont Correctional Institute. Williams said that Thomas, known as "747" because he was a high flyer, was a drug dealer who told Stephanie and her mother, Hattie Williams, to beat up Melissa for some dope that Melissa owed him for. They were in the basement of 602 Winans Avenue when Stephanie hit Melissa in the head with a baseball bat and Hattie began to stab her with a knife.

The day after the proffer, Ketler, who had heard about the plea and the proffer, asked Assistant Prosecutor Scott Reilly and Larry White if he could speak with Williams in the county jail. Ketler thought that there were some areas remaining unanswered concerning the murder. He received permission and met with Williams at the jail. His first question was why she took a life over dope. She stared at him for a period of time and said that she did not kill Melissa. Her attorney, Tom Adgate, told her to lie during the proffer and wrote out a script for her to rehearse. She said that Adgate did this because the prosecution was out to frame her for the murder and this would be her "out." She said now that she was upset with herself for pleading guilty to manslaughter.

Williams went on to tell Ketler that Melissa Sublett was murdered by Robert L. Thomas on the second floor of a house at 998 Baird Street. Her account of the murder was that she had gone to this house sometime in the evening on June 24. There were apartments on the second and third floors. The second-floor apartment was vacant but could be entered by climbing onto the first-floor porch roof and entering a second-floor window. Williams intended to go up to the third-floor apartment to see Linda Hollins. As she passed the door to the second-floor apartment, she saw Robert L. Thomas, whom she knew as "747," with two other men, his friends from Detroit, known as "Tiny" and "Lope Dog." She also saw, lying on the floor, rolled up in a multicolored rug, a body; one foot without a shoe was extending from the carpet roll. The men held a handgun on her, and Thomas threatened that if she ever told anybody, she would be killed.

Williams told Ketler that Vance Davis helped carry the body downstairs and loaded it into a white pickup truck belonging to Andrew Johnson. When asked, she said that the men from Detroit had a gold car with out-of-state plates. They were in town for some drug business with Robert Thomas. Williams said she wasn't sure the body was Melissa Sublett until Shawn McCoy came to Baird Street the following morning saying that Missy's body was found at 5th Avenue and Winans. Williams denied seeing either a knife or a bat when "747" and the other two men threatened her.

After her guilty plea, Williams returned to the county jail and, once there, said she told Summit County deputy Hale that she had to lie to get her three-year sentence. Ketler asked if she would take a lie detector test without an attorney present. She said that since she had been sentenced, neither Adgate nor Malarcik represented her any longer. She would take the lie detector test. The test was given on July 6, 1999. The polygraph operator opined that Williams used deception in answering the questions.

Melissa's body was found by the police on the sidewalk at 5:51 a.m., and the time of death was estimated to be after 2:00 a.m. My experience with lying tells me that people don't make up lies out of whole cloth. Instead, they take their memories and they tailor them. They add a little here and subtract a little there, enlarge on this and trim that until they have something that fits what they want you to believe. If they are really good liars, they start to believe it themselves and become amazingly convincing.

I have never had confidence in polygraph results. I think the better the liar, the more likely someone is to pass the test. Law enforcement relies extensively on these tests. Suspects who pass a test often face no more scrutiny. In some ways, the tests are the easy way to avoid a long and difficult investigation. They function for law enforcement as a shortcut to an answer—whether it's the right answer or not. The tests also carry the imprint of scientific certainty, which makes them a powerful tool to convince a jury. Defendants with a cocky attitude often are convinced that they can "Beat the Test." Sometimes they can.

The results of a polygraph test are generally not admissible in court unless both the prosecution and the defense stipulate before the test is given that the results—whatever the results are—will be admitted. This seems to me a fool's bargain. The results of a polygraph are the opinion of the polygraph operator. He or she asks questions and decides whether the answers given are true or deceptive. If a polygraph is indeed accurate, the agreement of the lawyers should not be necessary to admit the results as evidence. Their agreement does not transform an unreliable result into reliable, persuasive evidence of whether someone is lying or not.

Ketler learned the results of the polygraph on July 13, 1999. He also learned that Akron detectives had previously interviewed Vance Davis and were satisfied with his statement. They concluded that he was not directly involved in the murder. Based on this, Ketler decided to do no additional follow-up. Stephanie Williams rejoined the women in the penitentiary in Marysville, Ohio.

Stephanie Williams's statement to Ketler was not the first time law enforcement heard the name Robert L. Thomas in conjunction with the murder of Sublett. He was a suspect in the initial investigation early in June 1998. Robert Thomas spent part of that summer in Belmont Correctional Institute on other charges. Ketler and Sergeant Rodney Tucker of the Akron police went to Belmont to question him. On September 16, the two detectives told Thomas that they wanted to talk about the death of Melissa Sublett. Thomas asked if he needed a lawyer. Ketler replied, "That's up to you. At least listen to what we have to say first." Thomas responded, "I definitely will." Ketler gave Thomas his Miranda rights, and Thomas said, "I am going to cooperate fully."

Thomas proceeded to answer the questions. He said that he had seen Sublett but didn't know her personally and denied having anything to do with the murder. He told the officers that he was at 954 Owens Street with Anthony Johnson, Fred Jackson and Pam Stills on the night of the murder. Thomas said he found out about the murder when Gwen called Pam's house and told him. Thomas said that he later heard that in order to get out of jail, Stephanie Williams said that he murdered Sublett. Thomas believed that Williams may have had something to do with the murder.

In addition to the Sublett murder, the detectives wanted to discuss the felonious assault of Aundra Lidge. Thomas was quite forthcoming when asked about Lidge. He claimed that on June 15, 1998, he was at Queenie Brazil's house, 602 Winans Avenue. A woman named Gwen was also at the house. Thomas said Lidge attacked him. Thomas backed up three times before Lidge struck him in the head with his fist. Acting in self-defense, Thomas pulled an icepick from his shorts and stabbed Lidge in the stomach. Lidge turned to run to the door, and Thomas stabbed him again once in the back. Queenie ran out the front door. Thomas could see Lidge's car out front. Lidge attempted to run out the front door, but Thomas grabbed him and threw him down the basement stairs. Thomas said that he knew Lidge carried a handgun. Thomas went down the basement stairs and jumped on Lidge's head until he was unconscious.

Thomas saw a large amount of money and drugs on Lidge's person, but he denied taking either. Thomas went back upstairs and told Gwen to call the paramedics. Lidge's sister arrived and took her brother's drugs and money and then took him to the hospital. Thomas ran from the house but later returned and saw the police there. Instead of going in, Thomas went to Stephanie Williams's house, at 998 Baird Street, and took off his white jogging suit, a blue and white jacket and a black ball cap. He offered that he removed these clothes because he knew the police would be told what he was wearing and would be looking for a man wearing those clothes. The detectives did not ask Thomas what clothes he put on or why he went to Williams's house. He said he was aware that people used to hang out at 998 Baird Street.

Ketler and Tucker asked Thomas about several other individuals whose names had surfaced in the murder investigation. Thomas talked about each one. One of those mentioned was Marcus Brooks, aka "66," because he is six feet, six inches tall. He was a former boyfriend of Chrissy Johnson who hung out at Stephanie Williams's house. Thomas said that Brooks has a reputation for violence and was currently in prison. He said he also heard Brooks may have been involved in the Sublett murder.

Thomas indicated that he had told Nicole Czerpak about stabbing Lidge. Ketler asked if Czerpak worked for an escort service. Thomas said yes, that she worked in a brick apartment building on the corner of Pioneer and Goodyear Boulevard. Thomas said that he was willing to take a lie detector test.

The investigation of Missy's death grew more and more complex. Multiple people knew something. Accusations were made and contradicted. Thomas claimed an alibi that had to be checked out. There were some odd similarities between accounts of the murder and the assault on Aundra Lidge. Ketler was the only officer involved who knew about Missy's trip downtown to the courthouse two years earlier; none of the other investigating officers had been told. So, Ketler had more information about the various aspects of the

Sublett murder case than any other detective. But then Ketler was removed from the case. His supervisor in the Copley Police Department said that he needed Ketler to work drug cases. The murder investigation continued, but Ketler was not a part of it. Why would the most knowledgeable detective be removed from the investigation in its early stages? If someone wanted to impede the investigation, this would be a good way to do that.

Throughout the spring, Judie Bandy organized evidence, preparing more cases for the grand jury. The cases were presented, and on July 12, the grand jury issued thirty-four more indictments. Warrants went out and arrests were made. Because the cases were all related, they came to me. Once again Jill and I swung into action, setting appearances, appointing attorneys and trying to manage the tsunami of motions pouring in. Then we got word that the first major defendant, Laura Ridenour, who ran Touch of Class, was going to plead guilty to promoting prostitution, racketeering and money laundering. Jill set the plea date for July 28. Promptly, four more defendants agreed to plead to reduced charges.

By this time, County Prosecutor Michael Callahan was well aware of the claims made by Melissa Sublett before her murder. He asked the Akron

"Wow, she doesn't seem to be lying either." *Chip Bok*, Akron Beacon Journal.

police to investigate, and Detectives W. Rod Smith and Edward Moriarty were assigned. In what had to be one of the most efficient and expeditious investigations on record, the two officers filed their report on August 1— three days after they got the assignment. They concluded that Sublett's story was "unsubstantiated rumor," and that was the end of it. However, it wasn't.

Stuart Warner of the *Cleveland Plain Dealer* reported that Sublett's father, Mattison Sublett, said, "If my daughter had seen Callahan before, she certainly would have recognized him. She had been in Callaghan's courtroom on criminal charges when he was a municipal judge." He also said, "For the last three years of her life, she said she was afraid she was going to be killed by someone from downtown." He stated that she specifically said she was afraid of at least one Akron police officer and "someone who worked in the courthouse," but she did not mention any names.

SHE IS MORE TO BE PITIED
THAN CENSORED

On August 1, the prosecution took another proffer in conjunction with a plea from Deidre Longkamp. Deidre was an escort arrested after the second wave of indictments. While in the Summit County Jail, she said she talked with another inmate whose name she could not recall but who she described as a light-skinned African American woman. This inmate had been in the jail when the first escorts were arrested in February. The inmate told Longkamp that she had talked with one of the escorts, a "Wendy." She said that "Wendy" told her she previously had a client whose name was "Mike Callahan."

After this proffer, Judie Bandy started working to determine who would have been in the jail in February. The jail records indicated that Wendy Thrasher Moats was incarcerated at that time. Bandy said Moats was subsequently questioned but denied telling anyone that Mike Callahan was her client. Bandy told her boss. He denied any knowledge or contact with any of the escorts. Bandy concluded that this was just "jail talk." There was no significant evidence to link Mike Callahan with any of these women.

Once more, Judie came to my chambers. She related the circumstances of the proffer, the follow-up identification of Wendy Thrasher Moats and the denials by both Moats and Callahan. While this was disturbing to me, I was not terribly surprised. We had already had the "false names" inquiry regarding the four lawyers whose names were listed as clients in the business records. The fact that Mike Callahan's name again surfaced did not startle me. But I wanted to verify that there was no additional identifying information from the other defendants or given by these women. Bandy said no. I concluded that someone was using these names as a game when he hired an escort. Bandy left, and I thought it was resolved. She either did not know or failed to tell me that Mike Callahan was alleged to be a "mutual customer." Nothing was said that "red hair" and "judge or prosecutor" were part of the alleged discussion between Moats and the unknown woman in the jail.

More defendants pleaded guilty, and by August 2, I had taken twenty-one guilty pleas. In each case, I ordered a pre-sentence investigation report. This detailed report, prepared by the probation department, provides the information needed to craft a sentence. It contains the defendant's background, education, criminal record (if any), family, employment, substance abuse history (if any) and a statement written personally by the defendant about the offense. If there is a victim, a victim impact statement is included. At the time of sentencing, any victims who wish to speak can do so in open court. In addition, the defense attorney makes an argument, and finally, the defendant personally makes an oral statement. I do not sentence a defendant until these reports are provided to me.

Public interest in the cases remained high. The local paper, the *Akron Beacon Journal*, was at that time a thriving newspaper with a good reputation, some talented writers and a large circulation. The *Cleveland Plain Dealer* was the local paper to the north. Both papers carried accounts of the story.

The *Beacon Journal Sunday* magazine editor assigned a local feature writer, Bob Dyer, to do an extensive article on Jack Porter in the spring before any cases had gone to trial. The newspaper used large photos to illustrate proceedings and individuals involved in the stories. Reporters wanted quotes from the principal participants to enliven the copy and engage readers. One of the best sources for colorful quips was attorney Tom Adgate, who represented Jack Porter and other defendants. Adgate was witty, irreverent and fierce in his advocacy for his clients. He enjoyed verbally jousting with the prosecutors. His firm was Smith & Adgate. Larry Smith represented Julie Anne Bishop, who owned SkyeProm, and her husband. Her mother was represented by Andrew Kinder, another attorney in the firm. Larry Smith was also an experienced, savvy defense lawyer. He had had some rough days in his past and identified with many of his clients. Smith was passionate about protecting the rights of each individual and about making the justice system more humane.

But not every defendant decided to plead guilty. Taryn Chojnoski was set for a jury trial on August 11, 1999. The first major event in my courtroom was her

Larry Smith. *From the* Akron Beacon Journal.

trial. As in every jury trial, it begins with jury selection. Jury selection is part intuition, part guess work, and usually baffling to everyone. The process is called *voir dire*, which is French and roughly translates as "to see; to say," but I always told prospective jurors that it just means to speak the truth. Once questioning is complete, the lawyers may ask that a panel member be excused from service for a specific reason ("for cause") or for no reason at all ("peremptory"). One thing the lawyers usually want to know is if any prospective juror has read or heard anything about the case before coming in that morning. Have they formed any opinions about the case? If so, can they set those opinions aside and listen with an open mind? The intent is to start with a clean slate, with jurors who have no knowledge about the individuals or facts that will be part of this trial. Jurors who have formed opinions or have direct knowledge may be excused for cause and usually are. This is a fairly routine part of selecting a jury, but it took a twist in the first escort trial.

One of the prospective jurors who came that morning was Dennis McEaneney. He was middle-aged, a seemingly ordinary citizen doing his civic duty. But he was also a reporter for the *Akron Beacon Journal*, and he had reported on the escort cases. McEaneney had looked through case files, checked criminal histories and researched people's backgrounds through the Internet. You could hardly find anyone in the county more immersed in the facts and circumstances of the escort cases.

When I saw him walk in with the other jurors, I knew who he was and mentally checked him off for a quick exit. It was inconceivable that he would not be challenged for cause or be excused as a peremptory challenge. But it didn't happen. Neither the prosecution nor the defense asked me to excuse him. I was dumbfounded. We now had a reporter from the newspaper serving on the first jury to try an escort. He would eventually be selected as the foreman.

The only person more amazed by this than me was Dennis McEaneney. I could tell from his expression that he was in near shock. I administered the oath of a juror to the final group while carefully not making eye contact with McEaneney. In addition to McEaneney, two other members of the jury mildly surprised me. One was a retired sheriff's deputy and one a retired police officer. Defense lawyers generally do not want folks who have been in law enforcement on criminal juries.

Taryn Chojnowski was not a major player. Twenty-three years old, she worked as an escort. She sat at the trial table with her two lawyers looking slightly dazed as the trial began. The prosecution called its witnesses and laid out its case. Taryn worked for SkyeProm in an office in Cuyahoga Falls, Ohio. Her stage name was "Brandy," and she answered phone calls from clients who wanted to meet with the agency's escorts. She referred callers to specific escorts she knew provided the services required. That escort made arrangements to meet the client. Chojnowski also met clients herself.

One prosecution witness testified that he charged $6,300 to his credit card for four meetings with Chojnowski. During their encounters, she engaged in both sexual intercourse and oral sex. The business records of SkyeProm corroborated the charges to the credit card and also the amount of payment that went to Chojnowski. The witness identified Taryn Chojnowski sitting in the courtroom as the woman he paid for sexual intercourse. Another witness said he charged $425 to his credit card to have her dance nude for him and allow him to give her a massage. They were both naked, he said, and he massaged her breasts. He pointed to Taryn Chojnowski and identified her as the woman he paid. This witness was a man in his thirties whose discomfort at his situation was obvious. He kept his head down and answered questions quietly with as few words as possible. He disclosed that although he was married, he was lonely and wanted companionship more than sex. He called the escort service because he could not approach women in bars or other locations. He said that the prosecutor told him he would not be criminally charged if he testified and told the truth. So there he sat, sad and humiliated but not charged with a crime.

After these clients, the prosecution called another witness to testify, Katherine Shue. She told the jurors that some clients were served at SkyeProm's office. This was offered in order to prove that SkyeProm operated a brothel, a necessary fact for the crime of promoting prostitution. When the prosecution concluded its case, the defense called no witnesses, and Taryn Chojnowski did not testify on her own behalf. This meant that the jury would have to decide if they believed the witnesses for the prosecution and whether evidence had been presented to convince them beyond a reasonable doubt of each element of the crimes charged.

I never understood what the theory of the defense was. There are only a few defenses to a criminal charge. The defense in the Chojnowski case seemed to be "She is more to be pitied than censored." After a day and a half of deliberating, on August 13, the jury found her guilty of engaging in a pattern of corrupt activity, promoting prostitution and four counts of money laundering—six convictions of felony offenses. Chojnowski was acquitted of conspiring to engage in corrupt activity and six additional counts of money laundering. I accepted the verdicts and thanked the jury, finally making eye contact with Dennis McEaneney.

During the trial, the spectators' gallery had not been as full as I expected. A few lawyers with clients charged in the case had come in and watched for a while. Some curious folks and some courthouse regulars had been there. With McEaneney on the jury, the *Akron Beacon Journal* sent another reporter to cover the trial. Carl Chancellor wrote the news story that was published. He interviewed and quoted Summit County prosecutor Mike Callahan as saying, "We are happy that we got guilty verdicts on a number of counts. We hope it sends a message to the folks awaiting trial. They are going to have to think seriously about if they want to roll the dice."

Characterizing the justice system as a casino where chance determined winners and losers and a trial as synonymous with shooting dice was a metaphor that would come back to haunt Callahan in the months to come. My second escort trial was set for the following week, but I soon got word that the defendant, Heather J. Reed, would instead plead guilty.

Dennis McEaneney took his experience as a rare opportunity to tell the public what it was like to serve on a jury. He wrote a long feature article about his jury service that ran in the *Beacon Journal* and further enhanced the infamy of the escorts. After Taryn Chojnowski was convicted and the jury discharged, I told her to rise; I found her guilty or not guilty of each of the charges in accordance with the verdicts. She was out on bail, so I continued the bail, set a sentencing date and ordered a pre-sentence report. She looked at me as though I were speaking Chinese.

As more defendants decided to plead, Jill set each one on the docket. The prosecution took more proffers and added to the evidence. The second trial was set, but this was a trial to the court. A defendant could choose to waive a jury trial and have the judge decide both the facts and the law in the case. When a jury serves, they decide the facts and the judge instructs them on the law. Deidra Clark decided to go to trial without a jury.

The trial began quietly. Clark's lawyer, attorney Renee Green, was soft-spoken and seemed a little intimidated by the formidable Judie Bandy. In the back of the courtroom, I noticed two middle-aged women sitting together, looking distressed. Dennis McEaneney had returned, now back in his job as reporter. Unlike with the prior trial, this resulted from a sting by the Akron police. The arresting officer testified about the verbal cat-and-mouse game played between Clark and himself in the hotel room. He said that he wanted to know what he was going to get for hiring her, and she gave coy evasions. "You'll get what you get on your wedding night." This went on until the officer got a price and a promise of sex. The prosecution did not establish her connection to a brothel or "house of prostitution." They presented evidence of her employment by the agency and payments to her for her service and for other clients she arranged through the agency.

I found her guilty of engaging in a pattern of corrupt activity and nine counts of money laundering. I found her not guilty of conspiracy to engage in a pattern of corrupt activity or of promoting prostitution. I ordered the pre-sentence report and set sentencing for October 18. After trial, I asked Renee Green about the two women in the back of the courtroom who sat through the entire trial. She said they were Deidra's mother and aunt. She said that Deidra had convinced them she was not guilty. I suspect that having heard the same evidence I did, they were heart broken.

The next morning, Jill called and said that Judge Ted Schneiderman was there to see me. At that time, Judge Schneiderman served as the administrative judge. He came in looking bright and chipper. He said that he heard I had another escort trial yesterday. I said yes, a bench trial. "These cases are a lot of work." he said. "It must be really backing up your docket. Would you like to transfer these cases out? It would make things much easier for you. I could arrange to clear them off your docket." I could not believe what I was hearing. Never before had the judge been concerned about the size of my docket. Someone wanted me off the escort cases and had sent Judge Schneiderman in to try. I didn't say anything and just looked at him. He started to squirm. Finally, I said quietly that it wasn't a problem—I was managing just fine but so appreciated his concern. He beat a hasty retreat, and we never mentioned it again.

THE BLOWUP

For weeks, I thought that the case would blow up. There were too many people who had heard too much to keep this quiet. And then it did. On the morning of August 25, attorney Larry Smith asked to see me. He came in and sat quietly, hanging his head before saying anything. I could tell he was upset. He would not look at me. Finally, he looked up and said that his clients, Julie Anne Bishop and William Bishop, acting against his advice, were set to enter pleas of guilty the next morning. But he said that was not what was on his mind. He said he would talk to me about it the next day before their pleas.

Larry Smith was an experienced criminal lawyer who believed that he had seen a great deal of injustice over the years. His own life had been a rocky road, and he had great compassion for his clients and others who had not had easy lives. He was idealistic and wanted the justice system to do what it was supposed to do. Larry Smith was a courageous man who decided to speak out and act when others failed to do what he believed was right. It wasn't surprising that he shared a law practice with Tom Adgate.

The next morning, I waited in my chambers with my stomach in knots until Jill told me that Larry Smith had arrived. Larry sat down without preliminary chit-chat. He said that he had had tremendous internal conflict about talking to me. He had consulted with both Judge Elinore Marsh Stormer and the chief public defender, attorney Joseph Kodish. They both advised him to come forward with what he knew. So he was taking the risk. He had a taped proffer from one of the escorts. On that tape, she named Michael Callahan as a mutual client of one of the escorts and another prostitute. The witness claimed that this client had red hair and was a prosecutor.

I took this all in calmly, but I knew there was a serious problem. I asked how did this information impact the Bishops and their cases? Smith said that there was no direct evidentiary impact but that it was a serious issue for all these cases. I told Smith that no other defense lawyers had come forward and told me about this. Surely he wasn't the only one who knew? He said that all the lawyers feared reprisals. He was in fear of what could be done to him and to his clients. His livelihood was his law practice, and most of his clients were facing criminal charges in Summit County. I told Smith that I understood but that I could not take a plea from his clients at this time. There was too much I needed to know before I could continue with any of the escort cases. I sent for Judie Bandy and Brian LoPrinzi, and they joined me and Smith in my chambers. I did not want to violate Larry Smith's confidence, but they needed to know what I intended to do.

From where I sat, it appeared that material facts had been withheld by the prosecutors. If there was identifying information about any of these men named as clients, there was serious prosecutorial misconduct. I had accepted Mike Callahan as one on the list of "false names," which incidentally included Larry Smith. Was that the reason Smith was so conflicted? Was he afraid that he would be revealed as a client? But still, he had come forward knowing that it was possible and that there would be further investigation regarding the clients and their identities.

They left, and I called Jill into my office. I told her that I was going on the record and would take no pleas this morning. She nodded silently, left and apparently told waiting reporters that the pleas would not go forward. I knew what I should do, but could I legally do it? This was uncharted territory. Every time someone knocked on my door, the case got more and more complex and conflicted.

But I could not ignore what had happened. I had to act without delay and did not see any way out. I went on the bench and, with Larry Smith and the Bishops present, I announced on the record that all proceedings regarding all defendants in this case were now stayed. I announced that I would be requesting a special prosecutor to get an independent evaluation of the evidence and circumstances of these cases. I was issuing a gag order forthwith, and all documents, tapes, computer records/disks, unrecorded written statements and all other miscellaneous evidentiary items in the possession of the parties' lawyers were to be delivered to the court. This reverberated in the silent courtroom.

It was necessary to halt the proceedings in all the cases because now the prosecutor had been identified by more than a "false" name. He was implicated in committing a criminal act and had a direct conflict of interest as a potential witness and certainly a personal interest in resolving cases without trials in which the evidence would be politically damning to him. It also appeared that Judie Bandy had been withholding information from me to absolve Michael Callahan and had withheld evidence from the defense lawyers as well. This was prejudicial to the defense of these cases and a serious violation of the ethical obligations of a prosecutor. Until these issues could be investigated impartially, I could take no further action in any of the cases.

I went into my chambers and started drafting my order. I called Jenni Shuki, my law clerk, and asked her to start researching the appointment of a special prosecutor. Earlier in my term, the judges had signed an order appointing a special prosecutor in a difficult case. I assumed that all the judges would be needed to make such an appointment. I also thought Mike Callahan would fight it to his last breath. This was going to be a rough road.

One hour later, Jill told me that attorney Tom Ciccolini wanted to see me. Ciccolini came in looking obviously upset. He told me that he heard about the stay I had issued earlier in the morning and felt that now he could come forward. He said that he was appalled with what was going on in these cases. He was representing not only Laura Ridenour, whose plea I had already taken, but he also represented one of the escorts, Barbara Tepus. He said that the prosecutor was insisting that before any plea could be accepted the defendant must give a taped proffer. After the general questions from the prosecutor were asked, a final question was asked of each escort, "Did she have any information about any attorneys or public officials who were involved with any escorts?"

When his client was brought in to give her proffer, Detective David Smith was there to tape it. After Tepus answered all the questions, the final question about lawyers or public officials was asked. Barbara Tepus said, "Mike Callahan." Smith immediately stopped the tape and said that a separate tape would be necessary. He inserted a new tape, and the proffer continued. Tepus implicated Callahan and said that there were credit card records. She went on to talk about an encounter involving prosecutors at "Bill Goodlet's bar." Attorney Bill Goodlet owned a bar in Akron, and many lawyers socialized here. He and Mike Callahan were friends, and Goodlet also worked for Callahan in the child support enforcement division of the prosecutor's office. Ciccolini refused to say what was alleged to have happened at the bar. He said that it was too disgusting to tell me. Ciccolini asked Detective Smith what he was going to do with the tape. Smith said that it would be "handled properly."

Tom had done the right thing in coming to me, and everything he said would be held in confidence. I told him about the imminent stay order, including the gag order, and my intent to get a special prosecutor. I thanked him. Tom looked like he had just been given a reprieve and walked out of the office a free man. I turned my attention back to the order and began to make arrangements for all the evidence that would be turned in. I could hardly stash it under my desk. I had just gotten back to work when Jill said, "Judge, Tom Adgate is here to see you." I wanted to disappear—poof, gone—but I said, "Of course, send him in."

Adgate was the third distraught lawyer that day. He was ashen and could hardly sit still. He was aware of my orders and said that he was very torn about seeing me. He had consulted with a respected family member who told him to come forward. During a preliminary matter in Jack Porter's case, Tom had mentioned while I was on the bench that he would be seeking the disqualification of Judie Bandy. It was an offhand remark, and I asked nothing further. No motion was ever filed to disqualify Bandy, and the matter was dropped. I now asked about it. He said that it was a tactical decision he made and would be part of the defense in Porter's trial, but it was a "bombshell." He told me as defense counsel in a murder case that he learned things he could not tell me because he was under a gag order. I was stunned. A gag order in a murder case? What on earth was this about? I asked him if this was in a state court, and he said yes. I asked nothing further. Tom said he was so relieved that the matter was stayed. He asked about a special prosecutor, and I said that was my intention. He left looking like he just won the lottery.

I realized that this could no longer be just my case. I needed help. So I went to see the administrative judge, Ted Schneiderman. Despite his earlier attempt to get me off the case, I needed his cooperation. I told him about the disclosures from attorney Larry Smith, which clearly disturbed him. He said that he anticipated we would eventually need a special prosecutor. I agreed and told him that I would ask all the judges to sign the order authorizing the appointment. He offered to help where he could. I indicated that I also needed a secure location in the courthouse to store evidence as it was returned. He agreed, and we decided that Special Projects Officer Robert Gainer should handle it. It certainly qualified as a special project.

I returned to my chambers to sign the order of stay. Jenni filed it with the clerk of courts at 2:36 p.m. No going back now. Jenni told me that she had been researching the appointment of a special prosecutor and concluded that I had the authority to do it myself if the other judges would not join. I anticipated their approval, but this was good to know if I needed to go it alone. Then Jill came in with a disturbed look on her face. "Judge, Chief Justice Moyer called from the Ohio Supreme Court." I shook my head and thought, "Ye gods, what now?" Jill gave me the number to return the call. Jenni scurried into her office.

When I called, Chief Justice Moyer wasn't available, but his assistant wanted to talk with me. She said the press had called the chief justice and asked if a special prosecutor was going to be appointed in Summit County for my case. She said that she and Chief Justice Moyer had no idea what this was about, and she told me that she knew of no request being made. I assured her that no one had requested this appointment. She was so relieved and told me that she was afraid that they had somehow missed something important and that I was waiting for them to act. I let her know that I anticipated a special prosecutor was going to be needed, but the Summit County judges would handle it. She thanked me profusely.

I contacted our court executive officer, Robert Heffern, and let him know that Robert Gainer would be handling the evidence. We started planning how and where the evidence could be secured. I wanted the evidence from the lawyers kept separately from the evidence turned over by the prosecutor to ensure that all evidence in the hands of the prosecutor had, in fact, been turned over to the defense lawyers. I wanted no discrepancies and thought that it might be necessary at some point to inventory each individual piece of evidence to confirm that nothing was held back. When I found out about Detective Smith making the separate tape of the Tepus proffer, I suspected that that incriminating evidence would not have been provided to the defense lawyers. Evidence may have been laundered to eliminate anything implicating Mike Callahan. Jill brought me a copy of the morning paper. A black headline screamed, "Rumors Jolt Escort Trial." McEaneney wrote an account of my gag order and stay that stopped all proceedings until further notice. He claimed that there were allegations of prosecutorial misconduct. He wrote that Country Executive Tim Davis held a press conference the preceding afternoon and accused Prosecutor Mike Callahan of being "on the list" of clients of the escort services. Callahan was quoted as saying, "I can tell you unequivocally my name is not on that list." This was getting worse by the day. There had been a great deal of rumor and speculation

Tim Davis, Summit County executive. *Phil Long/Associated Press*, Cleveland Plain Dealer.

about "the list" or the "little black book." While there were client records kept by individual escorts and client records of payments, there was no master list and, other than a ledger, no "little black book." But the titillation of knowing the names of the "Johns" was irresistible. Now Callahan had been publicly accused. Where did Tim Davis get that information?

Bob Gainer found suitable rooms in the bowels of the courthouse to store and separate the evidence. He called Jill and told her where to send the lawyers when they came to turn everything in. He also told her that the prosecutor had brought nothing to him. Jill and I looked at each other. That was a fight we did not expect. At my request, she called Assistant Prosecutor Brian LoPrinzi, Judie Bandy's co-counsel, to ask him when they would deliver their evidence. She reported back that LoPrinzi was surprised by her call because he didn't think the order applied to them. Judie Bandy was not there, and they were not going to turn anything over to me. Jill told him the order applied to the prosecutor and that the judge expected compliance.

I realized that I was going to have to take this head on and quickly. I immediately called the sheriff to ask for assistance collecting the evidence. His office was ready to help but would need a court order. Jenni and I prepared the order and filed it at 2:40 p.m. that afternoon. Armed with my order, Gainer and two deputies went to the prosecutor's office. They were told that tomorrow would be better and that some evidence was off-site with CenTac. Gainer was not put off that easily. He called Judie Bandy while standing in her office, told her about the order and said they had to begin collecting evidence now. He asked for her help, and she refused. Gainer then started looking through the papers and boxes in her office with no idea what he was looking for. But he gamely stuck with it and found some boxes of evidence in the case. He and the deputy took the boxes and said that they would be back for more.

Meanwhile, Michael Callahan had contacted another Common Pleas judge, Judge Mary Spicer. Judge Spicer was one of the calmest, least political and most gracious women you could find. An experienced judge, she was capable and well-liked by everyone. She came in my chamber door to tell me that she had been asked by the prosecutor to mediate. I was in no mood to mediate anything. Spicer said that the prosecutors wanted to avoid turning anything over to me and wanted a solution that allowed them to hold on to their evidence. She said they were prepared to go to the Court of Appeals if necessary. They were adamant. I almost laughed.

I told Judge Spicer that if they wanted a fight, I would go public and the newspapers would fry Mike Callahan for breakfast. I also said that going to the Court of Appeals was their favorite threat and they should do it. This evidence was going to be securely held in a separate room from the evidence provided by defense counsel, and they had no reason to refuse to comply with my order. I wasn't going to mediate anything, and I also was adamant. Judge Spicer, looking very cheerful, said that she would deliver that message. In less than an hour, Jill received a call. The prosecutor would comply, but some evidence had been sent to CenTac and was out of their reach.

The fact that evidence had been sent to CenTac was another serious concern. First, it may have been the most sensitive and incriminating evidence in the case. Why would they release evidence to CenTac when trials were still scheduled and the cases were ongoing? I called Sheriff Warren. The sheriff was cordial and concerned, but he said he would need a court order to retrieve the evidence from CenTac officers. I assured him that the order would be forthcoming.

It had been a long day, and I decided that I would hold off on preparing the order for the sheriff until morning. Although the court closed at 4:00 p.m., as usual Jill and I were still in the office when she called me at 4:30 p.m. "Judge, Mike Callahan is here to see you." Callahan came in and sat down. None of his assistants was with him. He asked if I knew about Tim Davis's press conference. I said, "I read the article in the *Beacon Journal*."

"His name is on the list." / "Is not." *Chip Bok*, Akron Beacon Journal.

Tim Davis was the Summit County executive and a veteran politician who had advanced in Summit County politics, leaving in his wake the shattered career of at least one opponent. Davis had been going through his own whirlwind of scandal with two top aides convicted of bribery and kickbacks. His chief of staff and his legal counsel were rumored to have been having an affair. He had asked for a special prosecutor to be appointed claiming that the investigation was a political hit job. But his demand was rejected and the investigations continued. He blamed Callahan for prompting a federal investigation of him. "These prosecutors like to stick together," he said.

Callahan told me that Tim Davis had stated that Callahan's name was "on the list" of escort service clients. He wanted to take a polygraph test that evening and release the results. He said that he had publicly denied everything. He wanted to further respond to Tim Davis publicly but did not want to violate my gag order. I told him I was appalled by Davis's remark. I said I certainly understood Callahan's need to respond and that what he proposed was not what was intended to be restrained by my order. If he limited his response to answering Davis without going into other matters, I did not consider that contempt. Meanwhile, I was thinking, where did Davis get the information? How far had it traveled and who else was involved? Callahan handed me three tapes that were copies of the Deidre Longkamp proffer. He said that they were for me to reassure myself of her actual statements. I took the tapes and he left. I did not listen to them. I could do that later. I just wanted to go home.

DESPERATE MEN DO
DESPERATE THINGS

The next morning, I stood in the courthouse basement waiting for the elevator. A cheery voice rang out, "Hi, Judge." I looked to my right, and there stood Maurice. Maurice Terrell was one of the best people working in the courthouse. He ran the shoeshine stand in the basement and knew more about what went on than anyone else. He was always affable, and it was a pleasure to chat with him.

"Good morning, Maurice."

He looked askance at me. "How's it going, Judge?"

"Lord help me, Maurice. They are getting me down."

Then he shook his head and said, "They're just hookers, Judge." The elevator doors opened, and I got in, thinking of the wisdom in those words.

Mike Callahan had taken his lie detector test the previous evening. He called a press conference first thing that morning and announced that he had taken the test and passed "with flying colors." The report of the polygraph operator, William Evans, said that "no deception was indicated on any relevant questions" and concluded that "Callahan told the truth." Callahan not only defended himself, but he tried to defend his office. To do so, he had asked Sheriff Richard Warren to investigate any allegations of wrongdoing on his part or that of his staff. "The integrity of this [prosecutor's] office is too important to be held hostage by the criminal element that makes these allegations." Asked whom he meant by "criminal element," Callahan said, "The defendants in this case."

Callahan also had words for Tim Davis. "Perhaps now he'll follow my lead and take his own polygraph," he said, suggesting that the questions might focus on the scandal and bribery that have occurred in county government under Davis's leadership. "Desperate men do desperate things," Callahan said. I suspect he saw no irony in that. He said the news conference was intended to let people know that "I'm not going to sit back and take these shots. I'm firing back." He wasn't firing back alone. By his side stood his wife, Judge Lynne Callahan, an Akron municipal judge. The *Beacon Journal* published a photograph of the two of them at the press conference standing together, facing down his accusers.

Meanwhile, Tim Davis realized that he made a mistake and was trying to run for cover. He issued a written statement saying:

> *I would like to clarify a statement attributed to me in an Akron Beacon Journal article concerning the escort service trial in Summit County Common Pleas Court. The article, written by reporter Dennis McEaneney, contained a reference to me indicating that Prosecutor Michael Callahan was "on the list" of export service clients. I did discuss these trials with another Beacon Journal reporter, Steve Hoffman, who contacted me on an entirely different matter. We talked about the gag order that Judge Bond has issued that morning. In the context of that discussion, I did repeat a rumor I had heard about Mr. Callahan. I never made this comment as a statement of fact and never intended it to be treated as such. That does not diminish the impact the statement has made. I certainly do not wish to hinder what has already become a controversial trial. Whatever issues must be resolved and whatever evidence is revealed should be sorted out in a court of law. I am confident our judicial system will function properly in exacting a fair resolution of the issues that have arisen in this trial. However, I am more concerned about the impact this has had on Prosecutor Callahan and his family. There is no doubt that Prosecutor Callahan and I have disagreed on some things. That goes with the territory. But this is different. I would never intentionally make a remark that would cause pain to him and his family.*

But Callahan said something else at the press conference. There had been much speculation not just in the legal community but in the general public about whose names were on "the list." Now he decided he would go on the offensive, and he vowed that he would release the names of customers identified in the escort case when the cases in felony court ended. He said that he was making this promise in part to reassure the public that his name cannot be found among customers of the Fairlawn-based Touch of Class escort service or those of SkyeProm Inc., operating in Cuyahoga Falls.

What was he thinking? Weeks earlier, Judie Bandy told me that his name was in those records. Yes, we agreed it was a false name and not Prosecutor Mike Callahan, but nonetheless, his name was there. Was he going to say, "Yes, that's my name but not really me"? Who would believe that? Or had his name been removed? What about the Barbara Tepus taped proffer? Were they going to scrub the first tape and destroy the second one? Is that what Detective Smith meant when he said it would be "handled properly"?

Releasing those names would also mean releasing the names of other innocent men whose identities had been used by one or more of the "Johns." It meant identifying the four lawyers whose careers, reputations and families I had tried to protect. Was he lashing out without thinking this through, or did he intend to use this as leverage for intimidation? Was this why they had initially refused to hand over evidence?

Whether or not Callahan actually intended to release those names, people took him at his word. My phone started ringing off the hook. Jill was deluged with frantic phone calls. Most callers begged to have the judge stop the release. One woman harped at Jill to tell her if her husband was on the list. She was certain he was. She didn't want to wait and wanted to know immediately. Of course, the newspapers weren't the only source of news. The local radio stations broadcast the morning press conference, and a local talk show host had been following developments for some time. Apparently, he jumped into the fray to add fuel to the fire.

But I did not have time to listen to the radio. I first prepared my order to Sheriff Warren directing him to seize the evidence that had been delivered to CenTac. Now more than ever, I wanted it protected. Then I went up to Judge Mary Spicer's chambers. She was acting administrative judge since Judge Schneiderman was out of town. We had a regularly scheduled judges' meeting that day at noon. I wanted the appointment of a special prosecutor put on the meeting agenda. She said that she would and asked me if I had heard the press conference on the radio that morning. I had not, and she filled me in.

At 11:00 a.m., Phil Bogdanoff, an attorney in the prosecutor's office, called and asked to see me. I told him that I was planning to meet with the judges at noon to tell them the basis for a special prosecutor. Phil said that he would be right over. Bogdanoff had been an assistant prosecutor for quite a few years and ran the appellate division of the office. He regularly wrote and filed criminal briefs in the Court of Appeals. It was a specialized area of practice, but the law was well established in the criminal arena. The Court of Appeals may not have had an actual rubber stamp marked "Appeal Denied," but the effect was the same. It was very rare for a defendant to win a criminal case on appeal. As a result, Bogdanoff won practically all his cases. He was therefore under the belief that whenever he went into the Court of Appeals, he would win. He was accustomed to telling recalcitrant judges and lawyers that he would go to the Court of Appeals if they did not see things his way.

Bogdanoff had a proposal. He arrived in my office and started in at once. Prosecutor Callahan wants to move for the appointment of a special prosecutor for the escort cases. He is concerned for the speedy trial rights of the defendants. (Really?) I told him that I too was concerned with speedy trial rights. He said he was willing to give me a draft motion and an order appointing special counsel. If I signed it, they would not need to go to the Court of Appeals. (What a relief!) He also wanted me to keep this secret from the other judges—to *not* tell the judges anything, and if I agreed not to, Callahan would join my request for a special prosecutor.

Clearly, Callahan had decided that the political fallout from opposing a special prosecutor would be disaster. He wanted me to play ball. I told Bogdanoff that I could tentatively agree depending on the draft motion and terms of the order. I said I had to go to the judges' meeting, but I alone could appoint a special prosecutor if necessary. He left, and I headed to the meeting in Judge Mary Spicer's jury room. Before leaving, I told Jenni that if Bogdanoff brought any documents, she was to deliver them to me at once.

The meeting was tense. Two judges, Judges Schneiderman and Murphy, were out of town. Judge Spicer asked me to present the issue to the other five judges. I began with an explanation that I had the statutory authority to appoint a special prosecutor alone but that I wanted either all the judges or the chief justice of the Ohio Supreme Court to make the decision to appoint. I told them that I had reached a tentative agreement with the prosecutor that I would not disclose the basis for my request and that he would be given an opportunity to file his own motion in support of the appointment. I said that one thing was troubling me, but it was not a part of the escort cases. I told them that Tom Adgate had come to me very distraught about a gag order that had been issued in a murder case. He would not give me details but inferred that the matter somehow related to Jack Porter. Did anyone know anything about this?

Each judge denied that this case was one that he or she had handled. No one knew about the gag order. Then Judge Brenda Unruh spoke up. She said she recalled a case in Akron Municipal Court when she had been a municipal judge about two years ago. She said a murder case came in with a prostitute victim, and she thought her name was Melissa Stubblefield. The judge said she appointed Tom Adgate as defense counsel on the case, and it was bound over as a felony one, aggravated murder. She said sometime later, when she had been appointed to Common Pleas Court, she saw Adgate and casually asked him what had happened with the case. Adgate told her that the case had resolved with a plea to a felony three manslaughter but that he could not talk about it because Judge Murphy had issued a gag order. She concluded that this was the case Adgate was talking to me about. Issuing a gag order in an aggravated murder case was highly unusual, as was reducing an aggravated murder to a felony three. None of the other judges knew anything about it. I told everyone that I would give the prosecutor a chance to work things out and asked if could we meet again. They agreed.

Back at my courtroom, things were progressing. Phil Bogdanoff had met with the sheriff and Bob Gainer, and they arranged to hold the evidence. They chose two rooms in the basement of the courthouse and changed the locks there. Only Bob and the sheriff had keys. Evidence was being brought in, inventoried and secured. Phil gave me drafts of a motion and an order and asked me to make a statement on the record regarding the basis for a special prosecutor. His draft order made it appear that the conduct of Tim Davis was the cause for my action. I looked at Phil. He knew that wasn't true. I knew that wasn't true. I said I would review and revise it. Then he asked that the report of the special prosecutor be held in confidence. They were concerned that irreparable damage could be done to the prosecutor and lawyers. I thought, "No kidding." He said it should be necessary for anyone who wanted to see it to show cause. I know that once unfounded allegations are set loose, no way exists to undo the results. I said that I would agree to consider confidentiality once I saw the report. Bogdanoff left.

Before I could finish, defense attorney Don Hicks came to my chambers. Hicks was a quiet, self-effacing lawyer who had experience in criminal law and was well respected. He represented Wendy Thrasher Moats. I wanted to learn about the Moats proffer and the report that within an hour of the proffer she was in the hospital. Don said that in her proffer Moats denied any contact with Callahan. If she was the "Wendy" in the jail, either she decided to lie or another "Wendy" made the statements about Callahan that were reported—if they were said at all. Don revealed that Moats had given birth two weeks before the proffer. Yes, she was in pain when the proffer was conducted, but she said that it wasn't a problem and she didn't want to stop—she wanted to finish. A short time later, she went into the hospital due to hemorrhaging. She recovered. Hicks said there was nothing improper in the conduct of the prosecutors. The next attorney I asked to see was

Phil Harbaugh. Harbaugh told me that the only basis his client, Deidre Longkamp, had for making a statement about Callahan was the overheard jail conversation.

That was it for the day. I gathered up some paperwork and Bogdanoff's drafts and went home for the weekend. While in the comfort of home, I read everything pending and Phil's drafts. I redrafted an order authorizing the appointment of a special prosecutor and instructing him to investigate and determine if a conflict of interest existed for Callahan's office. I decided against summarily removing Mike Callahan from all the cases. To do that I would have to hold a hearing, and then matters would be presented to the grand jury. If in fact he had done nothing wrong, it would still be devastating for him and everyone in his office. I deleted all reference to Tim Davis. I wrote a memo to Jenni asking her to prepare two orders: one with signature lines for all the judges and one for me alone. The judges met again on Monday.

On Monday morning, I gave Jenni my memo and explained where we were in the matter. I asked her to give Phil Bogdanoff a copy of each order. The locks had now been changed, and evidence was being brought in steadily. I told Jenni that I expected a motion to be filed by Callahan requesting the appointment of the special prosecutor. We exchanged looks. I said that Phil would bring a copy to us after it was filed, and if I was in the judges' meeting, she should let me know. I then left for the meeting.

This time, all the judges were present. I told them that I had been meeting with Phil to try to reach an agreement. I told them that Mike Callahan would be filing a motion for appointment of the special prosecutor that day. I said that while I had the legal authority to act alone, I thought it would be better for the community if every judge signed the order. I told them that I still would not disclose to them the basis for the special prosecutor. If they signed, they would act on the motion of the prosecutor. But I stated that no matter what they decided, I would act.

Judge James Williams was the first to speak. He said that he could not sign such an order if he did not know the factual basis behind it. Either I provided that information or he would not sign. All the others indicated that they were willing to sign once the prosecutor's motion had been filed. I said it had to be all or nothing. If one judge refused to sign the order, it would invite speculation, and partisan politics would pollute everything thereafter. At that moment, Jenni knocked on the door and handed me the filed motion from Callahan and the two unsigned orders. I told them that the motion had been filed. I leaned over and signed the order that provided for my signature alone. I said that was the end of it. Jenni took the order out to file it with the clerk of courts.

Judge Schneiderman then offered that he tried to contact Prosecutor Robert Horowitz in Stark County to ask if he would serve. Judge Patricia Cosgrove said she had researched the issue and agreed that I had the legal authority to act alone but the prosecutor had a due process right to a hearing before an order was issued. I said that I thought the motion by the prosecutor waived that due process right. She agreed. Judge Brenda Unruh looked at the motion and said that she thought any report from the special prosecutor should be public and that Callahan's request for confidentiality should not be granted. I said I had not committed to confidentiality. Everyone looked grim. The meeting ended, and no one spoke to me.

The next morning was September 1. A black banner headline crossed the front page of the *Akron Beacon Journal*: "Investigation Ordered." The story was accompanied by a small photo of me looking smug. McEaneney wrote, "Judge Jane Bond signed an order yesterday calling for a special prosecutor to 'investigate the conduct of all parties in these proceedings, the state of the evidence and whether a conflict of interest exists for the Summit County prosecutor and his assistants in continuing prosecution of these matters.'" I was glad that I had decided not to unilaterally remove Callahan but would rely on the special prosecutor to see if a conflict of interest existed or not. I felt that this not only was fair to Callahan but also protected the integrity of the system.

SHERLOCK AND HOLMES,
AKA SPELLACY AND HILOW

So now I had to find a special prosecutor. There were no lists, directories or agencies that provided such a creature. Again, I was on my own. I called judges in the surrounding counties and explained my position. I got a few promises to refer someone to me. Then I decided to call my brother-in-law, Tom Wagner, also a lawyer and an experienced criminal prosecutor in Cleveland. Tom knew lawyers who practiced criminal law and those who had served as assistant prosecutors in the state and federal courts. Besides being a relative, he was a reliable, trustworthy source who would give me his best recommendations. We talked about the situation, and he mentioned a few possibilities. He agreed to see what he could do.

As soon as it was public that I would be appointing a special prosecutor, applicants appeared in great supply. Phone calls and faxes started coming in. I considered every one and was mildly amused at one lawyer who believed that he was qualified because his lack of experience in the area of criminal law would allow him to keep an open mind. Hmmm. The next day, a lawyer, Kevin Spellacy, referred by Tom Wagner, called. I didn't immediately return the call but called Tom to discuss him. Two other lawyers whom Tom contacted also called and left messages. Then I returned the call to Kevin Spellacy, introduced myself and told him that I wanted to be sure he understood the difficulty of the case and that he had the time to devote to it without delay. I generally outlined what I expected would need to be done—witnesses to interview, voluminous documents to review and scattered pieces of a puzzle to put together. He would be paid, but the hourly rate was not very much and this really was public service. I assured him that he would have my full support.

Spellacy expressed concern about the complicated nature of the inquiry, so we agreed to add one more lawyer, and he suggested his partner, Henry J. Hilow. I asked for résumés for both him and Hilow and told him that I would be asking about them in the legal community. A faxed letter and résumés came in later that day. I knew judges in Cuyahoga County, and I called for their opinions. Without exception, they thought he would do an excellent job.

I had a number of administrative matters to accomplish. I needed to secure funds to pay the two men and to locate an office in the courthouse so they would have a place to work when in Summit County. On September 10, I appointed attorney Kevin M. Spellacy as special prosecutor for the County of Summit and Henry J. Hilow as assistant special prosecutor. They were directed to investigate the conduct of all parties in the proceedings and the state of the evidence and determine if a conflict of interest existed for the Summit County prosecutor and his office in continuing prosecution of the case. My prior order required the special prosecutor to submit a confidential report of findings with recommendations forty-five days after appointment. It wasn't much time, but I didn't want this to drag on and I told both men that if they could not meet the deadline, I would allow more time. I swore them in. They provided fidelity bonds and began.

The next step was to put my own proffer on the record. I told Phil Bogdanoff that I would meet with Sheriff Warren, on the record, and set forth everything that preceded my order for a special prosecutor. I used this opportunity to bring Spellacy and Hilow somewhat up to date. On September 13, I met with both men and Sheriff Warren in my conference room with Sandy. I started my long narrative. To prepare, I handwrote a memo of the various twists and turns in the case. I taped myself describing everything I remembered up to that point. While Spellacy and Hilow took notes, I spent an hour reciting what occurred since the first cases were filed. When I finished, I told Sandy to seal the record until further order. I sincerely hoped that it would never be unsealed.

Of course, nothing happened without controversy. The next news flash suggested that I had asked my brother-in-law to "find" a special prosecutor. Reporters for both the Akron and Cleveland papers decided that there must be something amiss. The high-minded members of the press thought there was a suspect connection between Spellacy and me.

They contacted Judge Ted Schneiderman, who said, "I guess the discretion is with her." Attorney J. Dean Carro, a University of Akron Law School professor, and Stark County prosecutor Robert Horowitz were both called, and both said that I acted within my discretion. Regarding my brother-in-law, Carro said, "It's an indirect connection. The key question is whether Bond has any direct connection to Spellacy which she has denied." Other than that, Carro said, "She could appoint anybody." Horowitz said that the judge is in the "best position" to make the determination about bringing in a special prosecutor and that most special prosecutors are selected by individual judges.

When the reporter showed up at my door, I pointed out that I had to start somewhere. I explained the process and noted that I had received names other than Kevin Spellacy. I only met Spellacy as part of the search, and he came highly recommended with impeccable credentials. The final word apparently came from University of Akron legal ethics expert William C. Becker. Professor Becker said that he saw no conflict with the judicial code of conduct, and that ended it. So no fire—not even smoke.

After the special prosecutor's appointment, Larry Smith planned a meeting of the defense lawyers representing clients in the case, as this was an unprecedented situation. He wanted to discuss the possible legal issues and implications for their individual defendants. Many defendants had pleaded guilty, and two trials had resulted in guilty verdicts. What impact could the report of the special prosecutor have on those proceedings? Word of the meeting, of course, reached the press.

Reporter Steve Hoffman of the *Beacon Journal* called the president of the Akron Bar Association, attorney Dennis Bartek. He wanted to know if this meeting violated my gag order. Bartek was cautious and said, "If they discuss anything other than the generalities of the proceedings, it's not something I would do." He added I could find them in contempt of court. I told the reporter that such a meeting did not violate the gag order as long as Smith limited his comments to the court order and what was already public. I said, "I can only assume that he would comply." No one ever came to me and stated that the gag order had been violated or that confidential information had been given out.

The next development generated another banner headline in the *Akron Beacon Journal*. I don't know how the staff at the *Beacon* learned of the sealed proceeding in the Sublett murder case, but once they knew, they filed a request with Judge James Murphy for a copy of the transcript. Since there was no legal basis to keep the record sealed, Judge Murphy unsealed it the next day, September 17. He also revoked his confidentiality order. The explosive transcript became the source of major news. On September 18, "Officer Details Investigation" roared across the front page with a sub-headline, "In court transcript, detective recounts prostitute's efforts to verify story of sex, drugs. Prosecutor, target of allegations, cites tip that she accused someone else." Mike Callahan again fired back. He said that after the *Beacon Journal* report, a Summit County sheriff's deputy called to say that he had heard her (Sublett) talk a year or so before about taking drugs and having sex in Callahan's chambers but with a prominent defense lawyer, not Callahan. Callahan said that Sublett told the deputy she had sex with a defense attorney on the courthouse's sixth floor. However, the Summit County Courthouse has four floors. It's the Akron Municipal Courthouse that has eight. Michael Callahan was not a municipal judge at that time and did not have a courtroom on the sixth floor.

Callahan refused to name the deputy or the lawyer but said he gave a tape of the deputy's statement to law enforcement and asked for an investigation. Callahan said, "It [the tape] shows that she [Sublett] either made it up—or it happened to somebody else and she just changed the name to make it sound better."

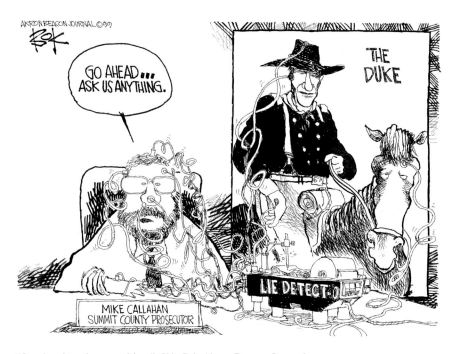

"Go ahead…ask us anything." *Chip Bok*, Akron Beacon Journal.

Of course, there are alternative explanations. The deputy may have decided to create or change a story he heard in the jail. Sublett had a long-term sexual relationship with a Summit County deputy who worked in the jail. Was that a factor? If the deputy who called Callahan had actually heard Sublett make such a statement, why didn't he report it at the time? Who else heard the statement, and why hadn't it spread further? Why didn't Sublett use this information to help herself in court? Why didn't she tell Detective Ketler? It was also possible that she had two sexual encounters, one with a lawyer on the sixth floor of the Akron Municipal Courthouse and the other with a "judge" at the Summit County Courthouse on the third floor. Possibilities are endless.

The Sublett murder and the events that preceded it had now joined the Escort Case. I was as mystified as everyone else until Detective William Ketler came to see me. I am sure he thought that the Sublett murder was behind him. He introduced himself and slowly told me the story of Melissa Sublett—the events from the time she first asked to meet him until the final day he was taken off the case. He related what had initially happened during the homicide investigation and the resulting aggravated murder charge against Stephanie Williams. Ketler believed that Williams had been involved but had not acted alone. He thought she was covering for someone, possibly her mother, Hattie Williams, or her grandmother Queenie Brazil. He knew that Stephanie Williams had not dumped Melissa's body on the sidewalk by herself and that at least one other person (if not two) was involved. Somebody was getting away with murder.

Ketler told me about Sublett's fear. She told him that she had been picked up by three officers in an Akron police cruiser. They had driven up behind Hoban High School to a secluded area. They had questioned her, but she didn't tell Ketler what they asked her. After the questioning, they took her back and dropped her off where they had picked her up. What was said in that police car? Why would they take Sublett—an average, run-of-the-mill prostitute and drug user—for a secret interrogation? Why did she express fear after the incident? Someone knew something and wasn't talking. Ketler was disturbed both by the death of the young woman and the circumstances that caught her in a web of deceit. I told him that I hoped the investigation would reveal more about her life and death than we knew at that time. I asked him to keep me apprised if anything happened that I needed to know.

When he left, I was more puzzled than ever about the death of Melissa Sublett. At the time, I knew nothing of the police investigation, witness statements and the multiple stories Williams had told to inmates at

Marysville or to anyone else. I only knew that Callahan was alleged to have brought Melissa Sublett into the courthouse for sex and drugs and that this allegation had so distorted the prosecution of Stephanie Williams that it was impossible for it to have been fairly resolved. How to explain the plea bargain that Williams had been offered—involuntary manslaughter felony three with an effective sentence of two years? A reduction like that from an aggravated murder, a special felony, indicated that something had gone seriously wrong. I doubted whether the facts could ever be impartially reconstructed and the truth discovered. Now I had to wait for the special prosecutors to do their work.

On October 4, another odd thing happened. An agitated Judge James Murphy called my law clerk, Jenni, and demanded to see the Jack Porter file that she was using. He sent his clerk down immediately, and Jenni gave him the file. About two hours later, it was returned. He gave no reason at the time nor any explanation later.

Although things quieted down for a few weeks, the case still affected the community. I received an unsigned letter that illustrated the depth of that impact on one man:

> *Dear Judge Bond,*
>
> *The purpose of this letter is to beg you not to allow the names released in the Escort Service Case. I went through a bad time in my life in early 1997 and late 1996. During that time I used the Escort Service several times. I admit it was a bad mistake. Since then my life is on track. I was married in January and have a child on the way. If the escort list is released and my name is on it my life will be ruined. I do not know if I can bare [sic] the thought of the public humiliation that myself and my family will face. I do not think that I can go on. Therefore, I am pleading with you to not release the names. I am sure that there are many others like myself on that list. Please do not let hundreds of lives be ruined because of 2 politicians bickering. You have the power to seal the records after this trial is over. PLEASE DO IT. It is the right thing to do. Not only is it good for all of those on the list but also their children, wives and families, and Akron and Summit County. No one would fault you if you seal the records for this reason. This is Akron not Hollywood.*

Of course, the women whose conduct equaled the culpability of the men they serviced had *their* names published. Despite the dozens of men identified in the investigation, only women were indicted. There is a predisposition of law enforcement to prosecute women for prostitution and rarely the "Johns" who buy their services. During my time as a municipal judge, I saw a weekly parade of women picked up for soliciting. Only once do I recall an Akron police officer—a very attractive red-haired woman—used as a decoy on the street to attract men looking for sex. The men caught in the setup were embarrassed but also slightly affronted that they should be charged for soliciting. I was puzzled that they thought a woman that good looking would be hustling on the street, but the thought that she was too good to be true never occurred to them. Of course, the "Johns" rationalized that she was a whore and that they were regular guys just out for a little fun. Cops should go after the real criminals. My anonymous letter writer didn't express any sympathy for the women who were publicly humiliated.

THE INVESTIGATION BEGINS

S pellacy and Hilow got right to work. The last thing I said to them after our meeting with the sheriff was that they were to go wherever the evidence took them. There were no sacred cows, no untouchables and no agenda. I would help them get whatever they needed, but I would in no respect direct their investigation. They were only to report to me when their work was done. As I expected, there was too much work to do within the time restriction. On October 25, they filed a motion for additional time. I granted it.

They started to ruffle feathers. One of the most difficult issues was the Sublett murder connection to the escort cases, if any. The only nexus I knew was Tom Adgate. Spellacy met with Stephanie Williams and apparently advised her that Adgate's representation of her ended when she pleaded guilty and that he was not representing her best interests. On November 1, when Adgate learned of this, he faxed a letter to Spellacy to advise him that his legal representation had not ended because Williams was still subject to possible criminal charges as a result of his investigation.

Adgate wrote:

> I was taken aback and outraged that you and your staff would suggest to Ms. Williams that I was not working in her best interest, in addition to saying I was putting Lt. Porter's interests ahead of hers. In the first place, the cases are not connected. Secondly, I am sure that I have Ms. Williams' interests at heart far more genuinely than you and your people. If I am wrong, I apologize, but at the present time, I do not believe you

are working on Ms. Williams' behalf. I am still totally committed to my client; I strongly propose a polygraph test to make sure Ms. Williams is telling the truth. In light of the fact that the polygraph has become such a popular tool lately, it might be an appropriate way to convince you. My point is, I do not believe Ms. Williams committed the murder of Melissa Sublett. However, the truth is very dangerous to Ms. Williams, and there is no reason for her to subject herself to possible harm without receiving something in return. That would be justice, *and the dismissal of the manslaughter conviction. If you are interested in this proposition and have the authority to right this wrong, I would be pleased to set the whole thing up with Ms. Williams and your team. It still perplexes me why you are involved in this particular case; however, if you in fact have the authority, we would welcome the opportunity.*

I have been at a disadvantage in sharing a few other matters I would like to clear up, and because of your inability to keep our scheduled appointment, I have not been afforded the opportunity. The first issue is, I was not *part of the hearing when Judge Bond stayed the proceeding regarding the escort case. I spoke with the Judge later on that same day when I was returning evidence that she asked to be returned. At that time, she said I might be getting what I had previously filed a request for—a special prosecutor. I responded during that conversation that I didn't need a special prosecutor; I would deal with the issue at trial. She questioned the issue and I indicated it had to do with Judy* [sic] *Bandy and Centac and I was not willing to discuss it any further at that moment. My issue dealt with the fact that Centac was withholding the information in the Sublett homicide case; not the information itself, but the manner in which they* [Bandy and CenTac] *were operating. That was it. I never mentioned Callahan or the allegations to Judge Bond. The only time it came up was when you asked me if Callahan had something to do with the murder and I responded, "No."*

After I received this letter, I called Tom Adgate and his co-counsel on the Jack Porter case, attorney Kirk Migdal, and told them that I wanted to see them and place certain matters on the record regarding the circumstances that were discussed in the letter. They came to my chambers on November 2, and with the court reporter present, I stated what had happened regarding Adgate's statements to me on the day I stayed the escort case and my subsequent meeting with the judges after learning of the Sublett case from Judge Unruh.

107

On the record, I said:

> *The Court: In this letter that I have received you state, and you reference that conversation that we had in chambers that day, and you state that you know of no connection between the Melissa Sublett proceedings and—Stephanie Williams was your client at that time?*
>
> *Mr. Adgate: Correct.*
>
> *The Court: ...and the proceedings in the Jack Porter trial.*
>
> *Mr. Adgate: Correct.*
>
> *The Court: What did you anticipate—what relevance was there to the "bomb" that you said was going to be part of the defense of Jack Porter? What connection is there between those matters that would lead you to say that to me?*
>
> *Mr. Adgate: First off, I don't believe I said the word "bomb." That may be the Court's recollection. I sure don't recall.*
>
> *The Court: All right.*
>
> *Mr. Adgate: I believe it's just—my sole complaint is the way they handled the evidence, not the nature of the evidence. That's all I was going to bring out.*
>
> *The Court: What links your defense—and we did not in any way have any substantive discussions in regard to the nature of the defense that you are going to be presenting. I don't understand why you referenced that to me or what linkage there is or you thought there would be that you could somehow raise something in the Jack Porter matter related to this. Is there admissible evidence here? What is this?*
>
> *Mr. Adgate: What we would hope to show is the way that Cen-Tac operates politically and then also the way they distribute evidence as they choose to. What they do, when and how they choose to make relevant evidence known to attorneys, judges, lawyers, police officers. It has nothing to do with the allegations contained within Melissa Sublett's statement to Detective Ketler. Just the manner that Cen-Tac does business and Judie Bandy does business.*
>
> *The Court: You believe that's relevant to your defense of the Jack Porter indictment?*
>
> *Mr. Adgate: I do.*
>
> *The Court: Any factual link that you know between the Melissa Sublett murder investigation and subsequent prosecution and the facts leading up to the indictment of Jack Porter and the investigation generally referenced as the escort case? Is there any factual linkage that you know of between these?*

Mr. Adgate: Other than the way they do the investigation is all, is my only linkage. That is all I'm alleging.

The Court: Now you state in this letter as well that you do not believe that Stephanie Williams committed the murder of Melissa Sublett. Have you discovered exculpatory evidence that was not known at the time of these proceedings?

Mr. Adgate: Yes. Subsequent to the—

The Court: Has that exculpatory evidence been presented to the prosecution or is a motion to vacate a plea going to be placed before the judge?

Mr. Adgate: We are still talking. I don't know which judge or prosecutor to go to.

The Court: Well, the judge who accepted the plea.

Mr. Adgate: Or what prosecutor to go to.

The Court: Well, I can tell you that the only—the only reason that the Sublett matter came to the attention, I believe, of the special prosecutors is as a result of what I told them related to what you told me. So the only reason to my knowledge that they have in anyway examined anything related to the Melissa Sublett murder stems from what you told me that day. Because you led me to believe that it was relevant to the escort cases and to certainly the defense of one defendant in the escort case.

Mr. Adgate: I believe it is.

The Court: You state in here that you believe Stephanie Williams is at risk. And as I understand it, she was in New Jersey in an institution, a penal institution, essentially for her own protection, and that it was determined that it was not necessary—it was not safe for her to be at Marysville as a result of information she has given in some proceedings, although I'm not sure what.

Mr. Adgate: I don't think that's correct.

The Court: Well, all I know is that I was requested to return her to our jurisdiction for an interview and that I signed a transport order and was advised that she was in New Jersey and that she was being housed in New Jersey. You indicate that you believe she could be subjected to possible harm. By whom?

Mr. Adgate: The perpetrators of the crime in the murder of Melissa Sublett.

The Court: Do you believe that she entered a plea of guilty to an offense that she did not in fact commit?

Mr. Adgate: Correct.

The Court: Did she do that over your advice? You were her counsel at that time.

Mr. Adgate: Correct.

The Court: Did she provide information that you believe was perjured?

Mr. Adgate: No. She never made any statements under oath.

The Court: Do you have information, specific factual basis upon which you believe further investigation should be done regarding the actual perpetrators of that murder? I mean, you indicated there has been exculpatory evidence which has somehow been discovered.

Mr. Adgate: Correct.

The Court: To whom have you brought that?

Mr. Adgate: To the officers working the case. Long before this broke.

The Court: You have discussed this matter fully with the special prosecutor?

Mr. Adgate: No.

The Court: So you are not—you have not advised him that you have this additional exculpatory information in regards to Stephanie Williams?

Mr. Adgate: No.

The Court: …All right. Is there anything further that you want to clarify or anything else you want on the record as a result of the questions that I have asked?

Mr. Adgate: No, other than—no other than I was not the one who came here to the court to request a special prosecutor.

The Court: No, I never indicated you did.

The Court: …Well, the Stephanie Williams case was over by the time you came to see me, wasn't it?

Mr. Adgate: No, no. See, they had brought her back themselves, Judie Bandy and Detective Ketler. They had run her through polygraph tests. They would do numerous other steps. And Don Malarcik and I objected to that, talking to our client without us being present. They said it was not about the homicide when in fact it was. We were completely misled, lied to, and we were hung up on the phone by Miss Bandy, each of us.…I felt it was inappropriate. I felt that's the way they are, that's the way they do business, and I felt—I was just outraged at the time.

The Court: None of that you recounted to me.

One month after Stephanie Williams pleaded to involuntary manslaughter, Adgate called Detective McFarland and said that Williams had named two men as the murderers of Melissa Sublett. One of them was Robert Thomas, aka "747." But that was not the first time Thomas was identified to law enforcement as a suspect.

Adgate and Migdal expressed more complaints about Judie Bandy and CenTac. They were not the only ones complaining. I received a copy of a letter dated October 31, 1999, from attorney Tom Ciccolini to Henry Hilow. Ciccolini referenced a discussion he had with Hilow in the presence of a CenTac representative, approximately fifty days before. Ciccolini expressed concern about the way the prosecutor's office conducted the Escort Case and its use of defendants to smear defense attorneys. He compared the Escort Case prosecution to another RICO case being prosecuted, the "Bump Shop," which involved insurance fraud claims for cars that were falsely reported stolen. He said that some car owners were actively engaged in the conspiracy with repeated involvement in the criminal enterprise but were not indicted. These car owners were people with authority, an educator with clout and Patricia Pry, a defendant in the Escort Case who allegedly had information about Mike Callahan. Ciccolini believed that the recent trend of over-indictment and selective prosecution was not right. He identified the root of the problem as almost omnipotent power placed with one prosecutor, Judie Bandy.

Day by day, my concern grew as the case was unfolding and revealed a growing number of problems. Then Spellacy and Hilow submitted their confidential report. They had centered their investigation on three issues:

- *Issue No. 1: Whether Prosecutor Callahan had been a client of Wendy Thrasher Moats as alleged by Deidre Langkamp.*
- *Issue No. 2: Whether any of the information provided to C.E.N.T.A.C. [sic] during the proffer and discussion with Defendant Barb Tepus involved the County Prosecutor Michael Callahan and/or one of his assistants, and whether such involvement resulted in either: (1) a criminal act; or (2) created a conflict wherein that office could no longer represent the State of Ohio.*
- *Issue No. 3: Whether the information provided to the Court by Attorney Adgate regarding an alleged murder case would somehow be relevant in the Escort Service Cases that would prohibit the County Prosecutor from proceeding based on either a conflict or an illegal act.*

The report initially explained the scope of investigation, the primary sources of information, what they examined and what they did not examine and the interviews conducted that were listed as Exhibit A. Issue No. 1 focused on the statements of Deidre Langkamp and Wendy Thrasher Moats. While in jail, Langkamp claimed to have overheard a conversation between "Wendy" and "Shelly" during which they discussed having a mutual customer for sexual acts named Mike Callahan. Wendy Thrasher Moats subsequently denied any sexual activity with Prosecutor Michael Callahan, but she admitted she had been in the Summit County Jail with "Shelly." No one identified "Shelly," and she was not located by law enforcement agencies assigned to investigate the matter. There was no evidence to support the hearsay-on-hearsay statement of Deidre Langkamp. Other than this alleged reference there was nothing to substantiate the claim that Prosecutor Michael Callahan engaged in sexual activity with Wendy Thrasher Moats or "Shelly."

Issue No. 2 centered on Barbara Tepus. Tepus was a troubled woman. She had had multiple cases with Summit County Child Welfare and lost custody of each of her children. She had worked as a prostitute for several years, operated her own escort businesses sporadically, been homeless and spent time sleeping on the couches of random friends. She was addicted to drugs and made wild accusations when it suited her. While representing Tepus in Juvenile Court, Tom Ciccolini had been accused by her of engaging in sex with her. She made this claim to a child welfare worker thinking that it could help her case. She promptly admitted that it wasn't true when it became apparent it would not help her. Tepus knew many of the escorts and happily threw them under the bus when she thought it would benefit her. She gave a lengthy proffer.

Barbara Tepus said that she and Patti Pry, another defendant, were at either Karams Bar on Wilbeth Road or James Dean Bar on Lovers Lane in August 1998. Patti Pry came with a man she introduced as Judge Callahan. Tepus described him as shabbily dressed, wearing a fishing cap, highly intoxicated, with brown or blondish hair and approximately five-foot-eight and 190 pounds. He drove a white van. The two women took this man to the Holiday Inn on South Arlington Road and used his credit card to obtain two hotel rooms. Then they stole his credit cards and later went shopping at Walmart.

The special prosecutors spoke with former Akron police detective Dan Kovein, who told them that in 1998 Judge Michael Callahan called him regarding a phone message he received in his chambers. Callahan wanted to return the call, to Barbara Tepus, but wanted Detective Kovein to tape it, which he did. Callahan then returned the call. She recounted an incident where she believed that Judge Callahan had sex with her and another woman, Patti Pry. She wanted him to know that she did not steal his credit cards. It was Patti Pry. As the conversation went on, Tepus described the individual she thought was the judge. Her description did not match Michael Callahan.

When the special prosecutors interviewed Barbara Tepus, she acknowledged this conversation and further stated that she knew the man whose credit cards she stole was not Judge Michael Callahan. When Judge Callahan's credit records were checked, there was no evidence of charges at the Holiday Inn or Walmart. Judge Callahan denied owning a white van.

On September 14, 1999, the special prosecutors talked to Detective David Smith of CenTac. They asked about the name Michael Callahan in connection with the escort services cases. Escort records showed that a male using the name Michael Callahan asked that an escort be sent to the Comfort Inn on South Arlington Road on October 10 and October 11, 1997. The records noted that a credit card was used. When investigated by CenTac, they concluded that the credit card did not belong to County Prosecutor Michael Callahan but rather to the son of an Akron police officer with the same name. Deputy Sheriff Detective Larry Limbert of CenTac verified the report on September 16, 1999.

Based on these facts, the special prosecutors concluded that the allegations that Judge Michael Callahan used the escort services were unfounded and untrue. However, the facts produced rumors that took on a life of their own when the Escort Cases began. Judie Bandy came to me to tell me that Michael Callahan's name appeared in the escort records because it did. She did not tell me that there was credit card information that identified another man.

Bandy did not tell me that there were details as to where and when "Michael Callahan" bought the services of the escort and paid by credit card. If either Barbara Tepus or Patti Pry had gone to trial, their allegations about "Michael Callahan" and the taped phone call could be used as evidence by the defense. Then it would be up to a jury to decide if, in fact, Judge Michael Callahan was the Michael Callahan involved with the women. He could be called as a witness, and his credit records and the tape of the phone call offered as evidence to rebut the allegations of the women. Clearly, he would have a conflict of interest in prosecuting these two women, and it would be in his interest to have them not proceed to trial.

But when investigated by the special prosecutors, Tepus and Pry had both pleaded and given proffers. So at that point, neither Callahan nor any of the assistant prosecutors had a conflict of interest. Callahan was absolved by the special prosecutors of having committed a criminal act, and Issue No. 2 was resolved.

The final issue dealt with whether the information provided by attorney Tom Adgate about the Sublett murder was relevant in the Escort Case and thus would prohibit the county prosecutor from proceeding because of either a conflict or an illegal act. The special prosecutors began with Tom Adgate's visit to my chambers and his description of the Sublett matter as having a "bombshell effect." They reviewed the transcript of Detective William Ketler giving testimony to Judge James Murphy; Tom Adgate and Donald Malarcik, defense attorneys for Stephanie Williams; and Assistant Prosecutor Scott Reilly. The special prosecutors noted that Melissa Sublett was murdered approximately five days after giving information to Detective Ketler. Adgate knew that Judie Bandy received the information from Ketler and that Akron captain Craig Gilbride also knew of the Callahan allegation regarding Melissa Sublett.

The special prosecutors went on: "This information <u>was not</u> forwarded to Akron Police Department officers who investigated the Sublett murder, namely: (1) Sergeant Ed Moriarty; (2). Sergeant Larry White; (3) Officer Rod Smith; (4) Detective Russ McFarland; and (5) Rodney Tucker. <u>These officers were never provided Lt. Ketler's report on Michael Callahan.</u>" At the conclusion of the investigation and after Stephanie Williams was indicted, these officers approved the plea bargain offered to Williams.

Assistant Prosecutor Scott Reilly told Michael Callahan about Detective Ketler's evidence immediately after it was presented to Judge Murphy. He stated that Prosecutor Callahan told both assistant prosecutors to prosecute this case the same as any other case. It is impossible to believe that Judie Bandy did not tell Michael Callahan about Ketler's trip to the courthouse with Melissa Sublett as soon as Detective Ketler told her in June 1998. She would never have withheld explosive information like that from her boss. Michael Callahan, when questioned by the special prosecutors on October 19, 1999, regarding the appropriateness of his office's prosecution in the Sublett case, saw no conflict and stated that all parties, including Stephanie Williams, were aware of the allegations. But attorney Malarcik's version to the special prosecutors differed. He said that Stephanie Williams was not in Judge Murphy's chambers when Ketler told them about Melissa Sublett's trip to the courthouse and that Williams never knew of the allegations regarding Michael Callahan. But even if Williams had known, Callahan should never have participated in the prosecution of Stephanie Williams when he was identified as a possible client of the dead escort. If Williams had gone to trial, Tom Adgate would certainly have presented Ketler's evidence, which would have been devastating to Callahan.

The special prosecutors added, "It is significant that the officers with the Akron Police Department who investigated this case were not provided this information, and the fact that this information was withheld supports the position that an outside agency should have been prosecuting this case. It is inconceivable that a law enforcement agency charged with investigating a murder is purposely denied access to relevant information. If the information did not involve the County Prosecutor, this information would have been disclosed."

But Spellacy and Hilow went on to state, "The *Sublett* case was not the bombshell described by Tom Adgate with regard to the Escort Service Cases. Ms. Sublett was not involved with either the Touch of Class or SkyeProm enterprises. She was neither a defendant nor a witness to any defendant under indictment in the Escort Service Cases. Attorney Adgate knew that there was no relationship between Sublett and the Escort Service Case. Mr. Adgate in his statement to the Court readily admits that he was conflicted between disclosing the information regarding Michael Callahan before trial or 'until such time as the case went to trial.' This information would not have been relevant in the Jack Porter case."

The report discussed the political nature of the circumstances surrounding the Escort Case and the relationship between CenTac, law enforcement agencies and the prosecutor's office. It noted that the investigation generated other inquiries relative to general practice and procedure within the Summit County Prosecutor's Office, but these matters lay outside the scope and authority of the special prosecutors. Spellacy and Hilow concluded with the opinion that the stay should be lifted immediately and the Escort Case recommenced. I agreed, and that is exactly what I decided to do.

WHAT NOW?

I did not want the special prosecutor's report to slowly dribble to one lawyer and then another. I did not want to show partiality between the defense bar and the prosecutors by letting one side have it before the other. So I asked Jill to set a status hearing for all the pending cases at one time. My order was filed on November 10, 1999, setting a status conference for November 17 at 1:00 p.m. I decided that the report should not remain confidential. It was important for the community to have confidence in the process. Transparency was essential. Since the prosecutor had been absolved, he had no reason to expect confidentiality. He would not benefit from a "cover-up," which is what it would have appeared to be if the report remained sealed.

I prepared an order of Preliminary Findings and Conclusions. I reviewed the work of the special prosecutors and reduced their work to specific legal conclusions on each relevant issue. They found that no evidence had been withheld by the prosecution or altered through omission, deletion or addition. One exception was the failure of the prosecution to specifically disclose the status of Katherine Shue as a confidential police informant. Second, there was no substantial, credible evidence to establish the identity of the Summit County prosecutor or any assistant or any defense attorney as individuals involved in any illegal conduct with any defendant. Third, there was a clear conflict of interest in the prosecution of *State v. Stephanie Williams* in Judge Murphy's court. Prosecutor Callahan and his assistants failed to provide substantial evidence to police officers investigating the homicide of Melissa Sublett; police officers failed to investigate allegations implicating Callahan. He could have been called as a witness in a trial. It was in Prosecutor Callahan's interest that allegations by Melissa Sublett of his criminal conduct not be presented publicly in a trial. Finally, the conduct of Prosecutor Callahan in proceeding with prosecution by his assistants under his direction prejudiced the administration of justice.

Fourth, there was no factual connection between the individuals and circumstances surrounding the homicide of Melissa Sublett and the indicted offenses in the Escort Case. But I found three links: 1) the participation of CenTac as an investigating agency; 2) the supervision by the Summit County prosecutor of both investigations and resulting indictments, particularly the participation of Assistant Prosecutor Judith Bandy; and finally, 3) attorney Tom Adgate's representation of both Stephanie Williams and Jack Porter.

I set forth standards for the administration of justice and stated that, tested against these standards, serious issues existed that required further investigation outside the scope of the special prosecutors. I was sending a message that I found major problems with the way the justice system was operating, but I couldn't do more than point them out. I ended with the conclusion that there was no conflict of interest in the continued prosecution of the Escort Case by Summit County prosecutor Michael Callahan.

The date for the status conference arrived. My courtroom was spacious but not enormous. It was filled wall to wall with lawyers and defendants in every seat in the jury box, at the counsel table and in the gallery. Standing observers and members of the press lined the walls. The atmosphere was tense. I took my seat on the bench, which is elevated and gives me a good view of the room. I slowly surveyed the crowd. Every eye was on me. I asked Sandy if she was ready, and she nodded. Stacked on the bench were copies of my Preliminary Findings and Conclusions. I announced that I had received and accepted the report of the special prosecutors.

I said that I would lift the seal on the report and that it would be filed with the clerk of courts. I announced that I would lift the stay and would set a schedule for each case. Pending motions would be heard promptly. Exceptions or objections to the report should be filed within one week, and a hearing on any objections would be set. My acceptance of the report was preliminary subject to objections, but the cases would move forward. I ordered that discovery be reinstated and all evidentiary material in the custody of Special Projects Officer Robert Gainer be made available to all counsel.

"Is it the prosecutor's job to 'make sure justice is done' or to 'roll the dice in court,' Mr. Callahan?" *Chip Bok*, Akron Beacon Journal.

Judge Jane Bond announces ruling, November 1999. *Lew Stamp*, Akron Beacon Journal.

Jack Porter, January 18, 2000. *Ed Suba Jr.*, Akron Beacon Journal.

I stated that the special prosecutors had identified three key issues in accordance with my appointment and their charge. I read aloud my Preliminary Findings and Conclusions. It did not take much time, and the courtroom remained absolutely silent as I read what everyone had come to hear. Michael Callahan was not in court, but I am certain he was the first person outside the courthouse to learn the outcome of the investigation and my conclusions. After I left the bench, Jill and Jenni distributed my order as the lawyers crowded forward to get their copies.

The press was brutal. Callahan should have been relieved to be cleared of the accusations against him, but he could not accept criticism of any kind. When contacted by a reporter, he deflected the criticism of himself and his assistants by claiming that I criticized Judge Murphy. He stated, "I think she overstepped her bounds. She had no jurisdiction on that case. What I see is one judge questioning the wisdom of another judge." This was a disingenuous attempt to demean me and imply that I had acted without authority. I certainly had no jurisdiction over the Williams case, but I did not claim to nor did I exercise jurisdiction by taking any action in the case. I never mentioned Judge Murphy. My criticism was of Callahan and the Akron police investigators.

Counsel for Taryn Chojnowski and Deidra Clark each filed motions for new trials claiming that Judie Bandy had not disclosed Katherine Shue as an undercover informant for CenTac. I set the motions for hearing on December 21, 1999. Before the hearing, when attorney Rob Coombs learned the basis for the motions, he went to see Judie Bandy. He told her that Ellen Kaforey had been the lawyer who copied a report on Katherine Shue identifying her as a CenTac informant. It wasn't until December 22 that I learned how Judie Bandy got the information about Kaforey when it was reported by the *Akron Beacon Journal*. The treatment of Coombs by the other defense lawyers when they learned what he had done was atrocious. Coombs defended his action by stating that it would be hypocritical to do otherwise. The defense lawyers criticized Bandy for withholding evidence, and he could not, in good faith, withhold what he knew. On December 10, attorney Coombs filed a motion to withdraw as defense counsel for Dea Thomsic, one of the escorts.

Lawyers gather at the bench, November 18, 1999. *Lew Stamp*, Akron Beacon Journal.

In his motion to withdraw, he stated:

> [T]*he undersigned believes that the atmosphere of the case had been filled with a lack of dignity, a lack of concern for colleague's reputations, and filled with behavior that does not reflect positively on our system nor our profession. The atmosphere has degraded to the point that the undersigned believes he can not represent DEA THOMSIC zealously within the intent of the Code of Professionalism. Furthermore, the undersigned represents William Clegg Jr. Currently another defense counsel has motioned this Court for a hearing relevant to information defense counsel has recently obtained from Mr. Clegg. This information is contrary to what the undersigned understood from Mr. Clegg. The undersigned believes he may have a conflict of interest in continuing to represent DEA THOMSIC in the event the undersigned is called as a witness in some manner. In reviewing the current atmosphere, the undersigned believes this may be a legitimate concern.*

This was the first I heard of William Clegg Jr., but it would not be the last. I allowed Rob Coombs to withdraw as counsel for Dea Thomsic and appointed another lawyer to represent her.

THE CONFLICT ESCALATES

While I was dealing with multiple motions in the escort cases, the Summit County prosecutor filed a remarkable request. Callahan asked Judge Murphy to return Stephanie Williams to the courthouse to give her the opportunity to withdraw her guilty plea. Callahan argued that while he had no conflict of interest in the Williams prosecution, my baseless and gratuitous public pronouncement that a conflict of interest existed could not be ignored. He further argued that her attorney, Tom Adgate, believed that Williams pleaded guilty to an offense she did not commit and did so contrary to his advice. Finally, he claimed that Adgate had told Williams to lie and had given Williams a "script" for her to rehearse for the proffer after her plea. He attached an affidavit by Detective Ketler, who had interviewed Stephanie Williams after her plea, and he said that she was now upset for pleading guilty.

Callahan asked Judge Murphy to examine whether Tom Adgate should be replaced as defense counsel. He stated, "Mr. Adgate has told Judge Bond and Detective McFarland that his client did not commit this crime. But Mr. Adgate did not filed [sic] a motion to vacate her plea and told Judge Bond he did not know 'which judge or prosecutor to go to.' Rather than filing a motion to vacate the defendant's plea, he intended to present facts surrounding this plea in another trial to help another client." Then, with no irony, Callahan went on to state, "The responsibility of a public prosecutor is to seek justice, not merely to convict. Cannon 7, Code of Professional Responsibility, EC 7-13." This request wasn't signed by the prosecutors who handled the Williams case, but instead was written and signed by Phil Bogdanoff and Michael Callahan. This attempt to remove defense counsel was extraordinary. Instead of riding out the Melissa Sublett storm, they were going on the offensive.

Defendants also went on the offensive. On November 24, Julie Anne Bishop and William Bishop filed objections to my Preliminary Findings and Conclusions. Attorney Larry Smith accused Judie Bandy of abuse of power as a prosecutor and said that her misconduct deprived the Bishops of their constitutional rights. He cited two incidents as illustrations. The first demonstrated her "attitude of win at all costs which is so pervasive that it leads to the belief in Ms. Bandy that somehow she is above the Court and that she is the sole arbiter of a defendant's procedural rights." He pointed to her refusal to comply with my order that she turn over the evidence in the Escort Case when the stay was issued. He said that this was but one example of what defense attorneys must deal with all the time when dealing with Prosecutor Bandy. Larry Smith wanted Judie Bandy removed as prosecutor.

Secondly, he cited the questioning of Stephanie Williams after she pleaded guilty to involuntary manslaughter in the death of Melissa Sublett. Bandy had told Detective Ketler that he could interview Williams without her lawyers being present. Upon learning this, Adgate and Malarcik faxed a notice to the prosecutor that Williams was still being represented by them and that she was not to be questioned without their presence or permission. Even after the fax, Williams was interviewed and given a lie detector test. Smith argued that ignoring defense counsel constitutes was a blatant abuse of constitutional rights and, again, demonstrated Bandy's belief that she could somehow circumvent both the United States and Ohio Constitutions. He went on to state, "This author believes that Prosecutor Bandy's actions serve another not so subtle agenda. She is letting every defense attorney know that she will investigate them if they cause waves or represent high profile clients." Smith also argued that Bandy withheld evidence favorable to the accused and that the conclusion that the only evidence withheld was the fact of Katherine Shue working as an informant was incorrect. He argued that other evidence had been altered or withheld by Bandy, and he sought to present evidence of that conduct in a hearing. My first thought was, "Why hadn't he told the special prosecutors?"

The second objection alleged a conflict of interest in the Escort Case. He argued that finding a conflict of interest in the Williams case also applied to the Escort Case because the allegations of Callahan's involvement in criminal conduct with escorts. As in the Williams case, Callahan had a personal and professional interest in keeping these allegations out of a trial. Smith argued that CenTac violated state law when Bandy and Detective David Smith orchestrated the investigation of the escort services and then failed to terminate the investigation when Michael Callahan was alleged to be a client. At that point, he argued that the entire investigation should have been turned over to the Attorney General's Office and the Organized Crime Investigations Commission. Larry Smith attached two affidavits by himself and Julie Anne Bishop detailing evidence that was not provided by the prosecutor. Included was the allegation of a missing tape supposedly made during a car ride when Detective Smith told Julie Anne Bishop that he had sexual relations with Katherine Shue.

This was of particular concern to me because it seriously damaged any testimony by Detective Smith. It was also extremely damaging personally to Detective Smith. One of the special prosecutors' findings was included as a footnote. It said, "In the matters that were brought before the Court, there was no implication, of any kind, of improper conduct on the part of the police officers, Sheriff's deputies or any investigators involved in these cases." Now I learned for the first time that Detective Smith may have had sex with a key prosecution witness. What else was out there that I didn't know?

The *Akron Beacon Journal* made the fight public. On November 27, Dennis McEaneney wrote a story that ran on the front page under the headline "Prosecutor Defends Her Task." Callahan defended Bandy and described the statements of Larry Smith as "whining." He went on to describe Bandy as "relentless," which was an odd defense considering Smith was saying just that. Judie Bandy also responded, primarily by attacking the defense attorneys. She stated that she had heard Larry Smith and Tom Adgate had been trying to obtain blank stationery from CenTac to manufacture evidence. When asked about this by a reporter, Adgate said, "Clever idea. I wish I had thought of it myself." But he said he didn't and that it was completely false.

Bandy launched a deflecting attack claiming that no one would care if the excessive racketeering charges had been leveled at African American drug dealers or convenience store owners involved in food stamp fraud. She said, "[T]his prosecution is stepping on a lot of toes of community movers and shakers." When asked, "Whose toes?" she wasn't sure. She did know that the "defense lawyers just wanted to get their clients off and keep them out of jail. When they fail, it isn't just a loss—it's a loss to a woman."

On November 30, the *Beacon Journal* editorial board weighed in with an editorial: "Judith Bandy, the senior assistant prosecutor in charge of Summit

County's escort services case, has responded to criticism of her tactics with unbecoming insinuations rather than answers." The board went on to recount her comments and concluded, "Like the charges of racketeering and money laundering in escort cases that should be about prostitution, Bandy's response is excessive and misdirected."

Larry Smith filed a motion specifically asking that Judie Bandy be removed from the case. He claimed that there was actual bias and prejudice between the prosecutor's office and the defense attorneys in this case. This was a completely different matter than the situation that existed in the summer when I appointed the special prosecutors to determine if Michael Callahan had a conflict of interest. Now the conduct of the prosecutors was squarely before me.

Callahan was also battling with Adgate in the Williams case. After filing the motion to vacate her guilty plea, he upped the ante with an affidavit from Akron detective Russ McFarland. McFarland claimed that Adgate told him that he (Adgate) told Williams what to say in her statement. Adgate replied with all guns blazing. He adamantly denied saying such a thing to McFarland, calling it outrageous, and saying that he was furious with the allegation that he had told his client to lie. He asserted that Callahan certainly did not have Stephanie Williams's interest at stake and that he was only trying to do damage control for his own actions. He said that he represented Stephanie Williams, not Michael Callahan, and went on to say that she did not want to vacate her plea. She simply wanted to do her time and put the whole thing behind her.

Adgate produced a tape recording of Stephanie Williams, now back in a New Jersey prison, stating that she did not tell Adgate what happened with Sublett until after her June guilty plea. He never told her to lie, and she did not kill Melissa Sublett. She chose to plead guilty to the lesser charge because she was facing a possible sentence of twenty years to life if convicted. She felt she had no chance. Sublett was white and she was black. She had no choice. This is consistent with Adgate going to the police after her guilty plea and telling them that two other men had committed the murder, not Williams. Adgate also noted that he was unable to find any legal authority for a prosecutor seeking to revoke a plea agreement negotiated and approved by him.

At this point, Judge James Murphy decided that he wanted out. He filed an order recusing himself, stating, "It appears that this court did not have all of the information on this case when a plea was taken, as much more was developed as to the circumstances of the offense." He requested that

Administrative Judge Ted Schneiderman appoint another judge—"some judge outside this courthouse, neutral and detached"—for all further proceedings in the case. Judge Murphy was so angry with me that he wouldn't look at or speak to me. I think that his anger was misdirected because he knew that he should have removed the prosecutor's office as soon as he learned of Sublett's statements to Detective Ketler. He tried to protect Callahan, but it backfired. The *Akron Beacon Journal* ran a large, bold headline: "Judge Departs Murder Case." Below that was the line, "Murphy withdraws. Police identify a suspect in 1998 death of Melissa Sublett besides woman convicted." Dennis McEaneney's article detailed Judge Murphy's order. But before the article ran, he had attended a hearing in my court to fill in the rest of the story.

"747" LANDS IN MY COURT

O f course, the Escort Case was not my only criminal matter. Fate had randomly given me the case of *State v. Thomas*—the defendant was Robert Lee Thomas III, aka "747," charged with the attempted murder of Aundra Lidge. The crime was alleged to have been committed in the same house on Winans Avenue where police believed Melissa Sublett was killed ten days earlier. There were seven other judges who could have randomly been given that case, but I got it.

Thomas was represent by attorney Thomas Shumaker. "Shu" was a savvy lawyer who represented primarily criminal defendants and had appeared in my court many times. His affable good nature and Irish sensibility made him well-liked. He filed a motion to suppress evidence. This type of motion requires a hearing with evidence presented before the judge to determine if improper police conduct has violated the defendant's constitutional rights. If the judge finds a violation, evidence, including statements made by the defendant, cannot be used against him at trial. Suppression of evidence frequently results in the case being thrown out. From my perspective, one benefit of hearing a motion to suppress evidence is that the judge learns something about the case. One of the frustrations of being a judge is that everyone else knows much more about the case than you do. Whenever I tried a case, I learned what happened along with the jurors. Only if a guilty plea takes place do you learn any of the facts.

Shu's motion hearing in the Thomas case took place on November 29, 1999. I came on the bench and saw Robert L. Thomas sitting at the counsel table with his lawyer. I wondered if I was looking at the man who killed Melissa Sublett. After the hearing, I wrote:

This matter came before the court for hearing on November 29, 1999 upon motion of Defendant Robert Thomas to suppress evidence. After hearing and upon the pleadings, the court makes the following findings of fact and conclusions of law:

1. In June of 1998 Defendant Robert Thomas became a suspect in the homicide of Melissa Sublett. As part of that investigation, Detective William Ketler of the Copley Police Department assigned to C.E.N.T.A.C., now acting Chief of Police, contacted Robert Thomas at the Belmont Correctional Institute on September 16, 1998. Thomas had been incarcerated on another criminal charge and was an inmate during the period of interrogation.

2. Detective Ketler, accompanied by Rodney Tucker of the Akron Police Department, interviewed Robert Thomas using a tape recorder to record part of the interview. Subsequent interviews were conducted of Thomas at the institution on March 8, 1999 and June 7, 1999.

3. At the beginning of the interview on September 16, 1998, the defendant was advised that he was going to be asked questions regarding the death of Melissa Sublett, aka Melissa Hunt but that he was not under arrest at that time. He asked, "Do I need a lawyer?" Detective Ketler answered, "That's up to you. At least listen to what we have to say first." Thomas responded, "I definitely will."

4. The constitutional rights required by <u>Miranda</u>, supra. were given and Thomas indicated he understood each right. He was advised that he did not have to talk with the officers, that he could consult with a lawyer and one would be appointed for him, that the statement could and would be used in court against him and that he could stop talking at any time he choose to do so. He indicated that he had one year of college and had been to barber school. Thomas was asked if he knew Melissa Hunt and he stated he didn't know but may have seen her in east Akron. He then indicated he had seen her. Detective Ketler asked him if he was willing to talk and answer some questions right now. Thomas stated, "I am going to cooperate totally." The questioning continued. At no later time did he inquire about counsel or indicate a reluctance to answer questions.

5. At the next interview on March 8, 1999 Robert Thomas was still in Belmont Correctional Institute. Detective Russ McFarland of the Akron Police Department again advised Thomas of his constitutional rights required by <u>Miranda</u>, supra. After advising Thomas of evidence that had been gathered regarding the assault on Aundra Lidge, Detective McFarland said, "If you sit here and give us nothing but denials about Missy…in a couple of weeks time you are going to have a visit from a Sheriff's deputy to bring you back to Akron to indict you for attempted murder of Aundra Lidge. If you completely cooperate with us today and I know you know what we're talking about, I'll tear up this in front of you and give you a promise that you'll never have to worry about this charge again. Got that now?" Thomas replies, "Yeah. I'll cooperate with you and talk." After more discussion of cooperation Thomas agreed to talk about the Sublett case and to take a polygraph. If Thomas passed the polygraph exam, the detective promised he would not be prosecuted for the attempted murder charge. After this agreement was reached, further statements were made by Thomas.

6. The third interview of Robert Thomas was conducted by Detective McFarland again at Belmont Correctional Institute on June 7, 1999. The tape recording of this interview is for the most part undecipherable. The detective did not advise Thomas of his rights to remain silent or his right to counsel prior to this third interview. Detective McFarland advised Thomas that Stephanie Williams had been indicted for the murder of Melissa Sublett. There were discussions regarding statements of others implicating Thomas and discussion of Stephanie Williams motives in implicating Thomas. He continued to deny involvement in the murder of Melissa Sublett. Detective McFarland reached an agreement with Thomas. The agreement was that if Thomas took a polygraph test regarding his involvement, if any, in the homicide of Melissa Sublett and passed the test, he would not be charged with attempted murder for the assault on Aundra Lidge. Thomas agreed. He took the test and the result was "inconclusive." Only if he passed could he expect that the attempted murder charge would not be filed.

I denied the motion to suppress.

Dennis McEaneney sat in the back of the courtroom listening and came to the conclusion that Robert Thomas killed Melissa Sublett. He talked to Detective McFarland, who told him that he didn't have enough evidence yet for the grand jury. But Tom Shumaker also had something to say. He told McEaneney that the allegations against Thomas were "ludicrous." "He [McFarland] is basing it on things he's heard from people in the streets and crackheads. That's all he's got," Shumaker said. The case against Robert Thomas for attempted murder of Aundra Lidge would go forward.

WHERE IS KATHERINE SHUE?

Thanksgiving came, and I was grateful that the Escort Case seemed to be moving. Lawyers picked up evidence, and Jill and I set trial dates. Meanwhile, another storm was brewing. The first week in December, Larry Smith filed a motion to remove Prosecutor Judith Bandy and the Summit County Prosecutor's Office from the Bishops' cases. He claimed actual bias and prejudice by the prosecutor against him as defense attorney.

Smith cited the *Akron Beacon Journal* article of November 27, 1999, in which Dennis McEaneney reported that Bandy said she heard Smith and Adgate were "trying to find blank CenTac stationery so they could write false police reports to bring to trial." Smith also cited the statement allegedly made by Bandy to the reporter saying, "Of Smith's claim that defense attorneys are being threatened with investigation by CenTac if they cause waves or represent high profile clients, I have no idea what he is talking about." There was no denying the animosity between Larry Smith and Judie Bandy.

On December 9, Larry Smith filed another motion on behalf of the Bishops to depose Katherine Shue and William Clegg as unindicted coconspirators and material witnesses for the defense. A court can order a prospective witness to testify on the record in a deposition if it appears probable that the witness will be unable to attend or would be prevented from attending a trial. The testimony in the deposition can be used as evidence.

When I received the motion, my first thought was, "Who is William Clegg?" I soon found out. William Clegg met Katherine Shue in January 1999 and became her boyfriend. He then became involved in the escort service.

His affidavit was attached to the motion:

I, William Clegg, after first being duly sworn, depose and say:

1. I am currently a resident of Belmont Correctional Facility, serving time for Burglary.

2. I met Ms. Katherine Shue, aka "Angie," in the early part of January, 1999 at 440 Norwood, Barberton, where she was living with my niece, Tammy Collins.

3. Shortly afterwards, she informed me that "Mike" who stopped by, was really a cop and she was working with him.

4. During the next few weeks, I got to know "Detective Smith" [David— not Mike] and agreed to work with him and set up some narcotics dealers, in return for having my probation/parole shortened. I was signed up as a confidential informant and given an ID number of 1067.

5. During the period of January through April, 1999, I drove for Angie, while she was working as an escort. This was known by Detective Smith.

6. I was informed by Angie that she was pregnant and that she thought I was the father. However, after the ultrasound, it was determined that the fetus was too far advanced to be mine. Katherine Shue then told me the father was Detective Smith.

7. In early April, after I had successfully completed a drug buy for 1/4 kilo of cocaine, Detective Smith gave me $350.00 which I signed for, and he told me that was the best he could do for Angie.

8. Two days later, I paid for an abortion for Katherine Shue.

AFFIANT FURTHER SAYETH NAUGHT.

_____*Signed* William L. Clegg_____

This affidavit was executed on December 3 and notarized by attorney Andrew Kinder.

Larry Smith gave a detailed account of what had happened in the motion:

In the instant case, William Clegg contacted this writer on or about Monday, November 30, 1999 and stated that he had information concerning Detective David Smith of CenTac, Katherine Shue, his former girlfriend and various other matters. This writer contacted Clegg's attorney and received permission to go and speak with him at the institution. On

William Clegg, January 2000. *Ed Suba Jr.*, Akron Beacon Journal.

Wednesday, December 1, 1999 this writer spent approximately one hour debriefing Mr. Clegg concerning what he might know concerning the "Escort Case." On December 3, 1999, Attorney Andrew Kinder again interviewed Mr. Clegg and attempted to verify certain information obtained by this writer. (See Affidavit.) This writer was asked by Mr. Clegg to hold off using this information if possible *since he was coming up for judicial release on or about December 22, 1999.*

On December 7, 1999 this writer received a phone call from Mr. Clegg informing me that Detective Smith had been down inquiring what he had said to attorneys Smith and Kinder. Mr. Clegg asked whom I had told and I explained that I had kept it a tight secret because of the sensitive information he had given me. We discussed his concerns over safety and the upcoming judicial release. On December 8, 1999 I inquired of Rob Coombs [attorney for William Clegg] *at 8:15 A.M. if he had mentioned the fact of my interview with any law enforcement officers or prosecutors. He replied that he mentioned it to Prosecutor Mike Callahan and it was in the context of Mr. Clegg's judicial release. Clegg did state that Detective Smith was very interested in the whereabouts of Katherine Shue. He also reminded me that he had told me that since Thanksgiving, Detective Smith has been "blowing up" everybody's pager or cell phone in an effort to find her. The sensitive nature of the allegations made by Clegg as well as Detective Smith's attempts to locate Shue clearly creates an "exceptional circumstance and it is in the interests of justice that the testimony of a prospective witness of a party be taken and preserved."*

Attorney Smith asked for all books, papers, documents or tangible objects be produced at the depositions. He also wanted the CI files for both William Clegg and Katherine Shue. He asked that I inspect the evidence to determine if it was privileged. On December 9, he filed the motion, and it became public. However, two days before, on December 7, Detective David Smith had gone to Belmont Correctional Institute and interviewed William Clegg. Why had Detective Smith decided that he needed to talk to William Clegg? He taped the interview, which was later transcribed.

Detective Smith asked Clegg if attorney Larry Smith had been to see him and if another attorney had been down to see him as well. Clegg told him that attorney Smith and attorney Kinder had both been to see him. Detective Smith wanted to know about Clegg's relationship with Katherine Shue and her whereabouts. What did the lawyers ask him about? Did they ask if Clegg knew Detective Smith, and did Clegg work for the escort service? Did attorney Smith bring up David Smith's name? When Clegg was asked, "What kind of conversation did you have with Andy Kinder?" Clegg responded, "He asked me, you, child, well I, if I knew how well you and Katie knew each other or whatever." Later, Smith asked, "Okay, did either of them make reference that CenTac was hiding her?" Clegg answered, "No."

Then Smith's questioning took a different turn:

> Smith: Okay, were you ever a client of Katie's?
> Clegg: No.
> Smith: But you did enter into a relationship with Katie?
> Clegg: Yeah.
> Smith: In fact, at one time wasn't she pregnant?
> Clegg: Yeah.
> Smith: We're assuming that was your child?
> Clegg: No.
> Smith: Whose child was it, do you know?
> Clegg: I don't know.
> Smith: You know it wasn't yours or she told you it wasn't yours?
> Clegg: Doctor told us, well doctor told us when she had the problems or whatever.
> Smith: Yes. How would he know that without the baby being born?
> Clegg: They done one of them things.
> Smith: Oh a DNA testing or blood testing or whatever?
> Clegg: No, when they run the thing over the stomach or whatever, I don't know what it's called. They put this jelly like on her belly.
> Smith: Yeah.
> Clegg: And then they run this thing over it and took a picture of the baby.
> Smith: Well how would they know by that that that was not your baby?
> Clegg: No they said how old the baby was.
> Smith: Okay.
> Clegg: Or how many, how long she was.
> Smith: Okay. So, so that would have, you're saying she would have gotten pregnant before you?

Clegg: Yeah, before me and her got in a relationship, yeah.

Smith: Okay. But you were willing to…

Clegg: Yeah, told her we could work it out.

Smith: Take responsibility for that child or do whatever…you need to do to make the relationship work?

Clegg: Yeah.

Smith: Is that a fair statement?

Clegg: Yeah, it's not the baby's fault [laugh].

Smith: True statement. Okay. Uhm. Did Kinder inquire anything else of any other inmates here?

Clegg: Inmates?

Smith: Yeah, here. Did he question you about any other inmates here?

Clegg: No.

Smith: Did he mention CenTac or did he mention law enforcement or Summit County or myself? Did…

Clegg: He just asked me if I had talked to anybody from, you know any cops and I said no.

Smith: At any time during either of the interviews with either Larry Smith or Andy Kinder did you ever indicate to them that you knew that I was involved in a sexual relationship with Katherine Shue or Angie?

Clegg: They never asked me.

Officer Smith was clearly trying to find out what Shue had told Clegg and how much Clegg revealed to the lawyers or anyone else about Smith and Shue's sexual relationship. Smith didn't go to the prison to interview Clegg about the case—he went to find out what the lawyers now knew about him.

THE JUSTICE SYSTEM ON TRIAL

While I was under siege in the Escort Case, Tom Adgate and Mike Callahan continued the battle over Stephanie Williams. Judge Ted Schneiderman needed to replace Judge Murphy. He asked Judge Jerry Hayes to come in as a visiting judge in the case. Judge Hayes served in rural Portage County to the east of Summit County. He was an affable man who was part of a small legal community where everyone knew everyone else and major crimes were few and far between. He could not have been happy to have this contretemps in his lap.

On December 4, the *Akron Beacon Journal* ran a story by Margaret Newkirk that began, "If it's Friday, it must be the defense." She likened the multiple motions to a series of shots fired between defense attorneys and the prosecutor's office. She reviewed the latest volleys. Callahan had filed a motion asking that Williams be given an opportunity to withdraw her guilty plea and that Adgate be removed from the case. In a taped conversation with Adgate, Williams said, "I do not want to come back to the county jail and I do not want to withdraw my guilty plea."

Adgate asked Judge Hayes to dismiss Callahan's request. He wrote, "What part of 'I don't want to withdraw my guilty plea'…does Prosecutor Callahan not understand?" His motion also accused Callahan of wasting taxpayer money on malicious efforts to strike out at attorney Adgate, and Callahan seemed confused about his role in the legal system. By seeking a hearing that would allow Williams to withdraw her plea; "Callahan was acting like a defense attorney—and not a very good one." Adgate concluded, "If

Prosecutor Callahan wants to step in the shoes of Stephanie Williams, then I would make a motion to have my new client examined for competency."

Callahan made a slight gesture of rising above the fray and said that he would not dignify Adgate's newest filing with a response other than to say it was "bull." He added that Adgate had used the clerk of courts' office "as a venue for having a press conference. It shows his character." Judge Hayes reviewed all this, and on December 30, 1999, he issued an order denying the request to return Stephanie Williams to Summit County. This battle was over, and Adgate won. Callahan limped off the field.

On December 11, 1999, the *Cleveland Plain Dealer* published a major article about the Escort Case. Under the headline "Call-Girl Case Upends County Justice System," it ran large photos of Donald Fulkerson, Tom Adgate, Michael Callahan and me. The reporter was Stuart Warner, a former *Akron Beacon Journal* reporter who relocated to the rival paper in the north. Warner interviewed Akron Bar Association president Carmen Roberto, who said, "This case has become far too personal. People are shaking their heads at the perceived damage this has done to our legal community." Warner brought up the costs incurred in the lengthy investigation by CenTac, the fees of defense lawyers and the costs of prosecution. But Roberto said that he worried the cost had been much greater than dollars and cents. "The bottom line is that this is a prostitution case. Not a murder. Not a serious bank robbery. I don't think the effort will be worth the results…not in light of all the harm it may do to the public confidence in the judicial system."

The article reviewed the highlights of the case since its inception with CenTac. One aspect that had gained increasing attention in the articles and editorials was the use of the RICO statutes to enhance the charges and the potential penalties. Warner quoted Tom Adgate, who called the racketeering charges "truly outrageous. These were not major crime operations. They were hookers with telephones.…They're being charged with more serious crimes than Al Capone was ever convicted of." Warner noted that the two women who had been convicted faced sentences in prison up to thirty years. It was because the RICO indictments carried such lengthy sentences that the defendants had so much at stake. Knowing that, defense lawyers were determined to do everything possible to defend against what they saw as egregious overreach by CenTac and the prosecutors.

To do that, Larry Smith intended to put the criminal justice system on trial. On December 17, he filed his witness list for the trial of Julie Anne Bishop. It included six Akron police officers; four deputy sheriffs; three judges, Judge Kim Hoover, Judge James Murphy and Judge Ted Schneiderman; Prosecutor

Michael Callahan; Dan Kovein; Detective William Ketler; law professor J. Dean Carro; law professor Wilson Huhn; Robert Gainer; Katherine Shue; William Clegg; Laura Ridenour; Deidre Langkamp; Assistant Prosecutor Judith Bandy; Douglas Prade; attorney Peter T. Cahoon; attorney Thomas A. Ciccolini; attorney Renee Green; attorney Ellen Kaforey; attorney Debra Migdal; attorney William Whitaker; and attorney Robert Coombs.

I wondered what the impact of this list would be in the Prosecutor's Office. Bad press in letters to the editor, editorial criticism and continuing developments made CenTac and Bandy look worse and worse. The possibility of CenTac's money being used to pay for an abortion by a prostitute, allegedly pregnant with the child of the police officer who was leading Operation Red Light, had yet to hit the front page, but I knew that it would.

Next up for me was a hearing on the new trial motions of Taryn Chojnowski and Deidra Clark. I set December 21 for hearings on multiple motions in the case. The attorneys for Chojnowski, Ellen Kaforey and Constance Hesske, came back to court arguing that they should have been told that Katherine Shue was an informant because her testimony was necessary to prove that the SkyeProm office was used as a brothel. Bandy was ready for them. She laid out the informal procedure that the defense lawyers used under Tom Adgate's leadership. Each lawyer reviewed a portion of the evidence in the files in the prosecutor's office and shared the notes. Then Bandy said that the documents that identified Katherine Shue as an informant had been copied by—she paused dramatically—Ellen Kaforey, the attorney for Taryn Chojnowski. Kaforey looked like she had been hit by a brick. She did not, however, deny what Bandy had said. Needless to say, I denied the motion for a new trial. I also denied the motion for a new trial for Deidra Clark because she had not been found guilty of the charge requiring proof of a brothel.

As part of the hearing, Judie Bandy produced the investigative files on Clark and Chojnowski. I admitted them as evidence. The files were large, and they were left on the bailiff's desk in the courtroom when the hearing ended late in the afternoon. As evidence, they become public records and available to the press. But most of the reporters who were present at the hearing paid no attention to them and left. Only one reporter, Eric Mansfield from WKYC (Channel 3), remained. He examined the files that contained the names of many of the clients. One black folder was part of the stack. I was not in the courtroom when his camera man started filming. I asked Jill to bring me the documents to use in writing my decision. After Eric Mansfield and his camera man left, she collected everything.

That evening, the broadcast on WKYC referred to the black folder as the "black book" of client names. Although the station did not name any clients, reporters, with cameras rolling, knocked on the doors of some of the people whose names were reportedly on the list. I did not see the news report on Channel 3, but the next morning I certainly heard about it.

The first thing I found when I arrived was *Akron Beacon Journal* reporter Margaret Newkirk, waiting for me, and she was upset. She demanded to see the evidence from the hearing the day before and accused me of letting Eric Mansfield see it and no one else. I calmly pointed out that it sat in the courtroom after the hearing and that she or anyone else could have looked at it. She didn't and Eric Mansfield did. It was that simple. I further said that I had the evidence in my chambers because I was using it. No, she could not see it.

I suspect that she got called on the carpet by her editor when Eric Mansfield scooped all the other news media with his story. She had no one to blame but herself. I was disgusted when I learned that the station had sensationally reported that the Escort Case client list had been disclosed. I did not know that any client names were in the documents admitted as evidence. But the "list" had not been disclosed. Mansfield jotted down some names and addresses and used those to stage the door knocking but revealed no identities. However, the *Akron Beacon Journal* wanted those files, and they promptly filed a public document request to get them.

The voluminous file was now in my office, and I began going through it. I withdrew the client names that I was not going to release. I also discovered a transcript of Detective Ketler's September 1998 interview with Robert Thomas. Why was evidence in the Sublett murder in the escort files? Someone thought that the cases were linked.

A NEW MILLENNIUM AND A
NEW PROSECUTOR

The year 2000 arrived without catastrophic computer meltdowns, power failures or a return to the Dark Ages. For the Escort Case, it brought a new prosecutor. His name was Charles E. Kirkwood. I would like to think that this change was in response to the significant issues in the cases and the pursuit of justice—but maybe not. Michael Callahan was up for election in November, and he had to have been suffering each time a news article or editorial about the Escort Case was published. He certainly knew that he had a brutal race ahead. He also might have a primary—if a Republican filed to run against him. He could be assured of a Democratic opponent in November, but he didn't want primary opposition. Tom Adgate, a registered Republican, let it be known that he was considering a run against Callahan in the March primary. I suspect—pure speculation—that these realities were the impetus for Callahan taking a drastic step. He brought in Charles Kirkwood as chief assistant prosecutor of the Criminal Division.

I first met Kirkwood in the late 1970s when I was an assistant prosecuting attorney in Summit County. He was a large man and not particular about his appearance, wearing inexpensive, baggy suits, giving him a perpetually rumpled appearence. But he was skilled in the courtroom, and juries loved him. He was shrewd and intelligent and his knowledge of criminal law was exceptional. He could analyze facts and knew exactly how a case could be won or lost He was a Democrat who left the prosecutor's office when his boss, Stephan Gabalac, lost reelection.

Charles Kirkwood, January 18, 2000. *Ed Suba Jr.*, Akron Beacon Journal.

When Kirkwood left Summit County, he went on to work as chief of the Criminal Division in the Portage County Prosecutor's Office and then, in 1981, took a position with the University of Akron School of Law. He flourished in academia. He was highly respected and named Professor of the Year in 1983. He left in 1994. I have no idea who, if anyone, suggested to Mike Callahan that he ask Kirkwood to join his office as chief assistant prosecutor of the Criminal Division. It was a brilliant move. I suspect—again pure speculation—that Callahan would have promised Kirkwood he would have freedom to use his own judgment. He would consult with Callahan but maintain his professional independence. I wasn't privy to the uproar this probably caused with CenTac and within his office. But it was a game changer. How humiliating for Judie Bandy that Kirkwood arrived to personally handle the Escort Case.

Meanwhile, I had issues I had to address. The first problem was Larry Smith's request to depose Katherine Shue and William Clegg. Ohio Criminal Rule 15 states that if it appears probable that a prospective witness will be unable to attend or will be prevented from attending a trial and his testimony is material, the court can order that his testimony be taken by deposition, if necessary, to prevent a failure of justice. This was what Smith was asking me to do. He wanted to question both Clegg and Shue under oath so that he could use their statements as evidence at Bishop's trial if necessary. I could only allow depositions if Katherine Shue and William Clegg were likely to be unable to attend the trial and testify or would be prevented from attending and testifying. This was sticky. At the time, Katherine Shue's whereabouts were unknown—despite efforts to find her. If I allowed Smith to depose her, she had to have notice of the time and location of the deposition. I couldn't do that if I didn't know where she was. William Clegg was in prison and could be subpoenaed into court by the defense. He was not unable to appear nor would he be prevented from testifying at trial. While I understood the problem Smith faced, I could not grant the motion.

Sometimes something happens for which there is no logical explanation. Serendipity is a wonderful concept. I kept on my desk a hefty handbook containing all the criminal law statutes and criminal rules of procedure for the State of Ohio. I was pondering what, if anything, I could do about Shue and Clegg, and I casually opened my handbook and glanced at it. I saw a statute that I did not know existed and was exactly what I needed. I was gobsmacked. I read it twice. It was Revised Code Section 2945.50. The statute provided that if an indictment is pending, either the prosecution or defendant could apply to the court for a commission to take the deposition of any witness. The court could grant a commission and make an order stating in what manner and for what length of time notice shall be given to the prosecution or the defense before the witness is examined. I didn't need my law clerk. I started a draft order. I needed a special collateral proceeding to establish the grounds and conducted it on January 3, 2000. I contacted Kevin Spellacy and told him what I needed and asked when he was available to come to conduct depositions. He said January 14, 2000, was fine. On January 6, I issued an order of deposition and appointment of commission. This amazing statute authorized the deposition of a potential witness by commission. Eureka!

I ordered that William Clegg be transported from prison to appear on January 14, and I issued a subpoena for Katherine Shue to appear in my courtroom at the same time. I ordered that any individual with knowledge of the whereabouts of Katherine Shue report such information to the court or to the sheriff immediately. If CenTac officers were, in fact, hiding Katherine Shue, as Detective Smith had asked of William Clegg, they were now subject to contempt of court if they failed to disclose her location. This order went to the prosecutor, all defense counsel, attorney Robert Coombs for William Clegg, the sheriff and the two special prosecutors. My subpoenas were filed the same day, January 6. January 14, 2000, was likely to be a red-letter day in the Escort Case.

The next day, the *Akron Beacon Journal* ran the story. The headline was "Judge Wants Allegations Explored." For the first time, Margaret Newkirk reported on the affidavit Larry Smith filed in which William Clegg alleged Katherine Shue was pregnant and Detective Smith used CenTac money to pay for Shue's abortion. She zeroed in on the part of my order that referenced an investigation of Detective Smith. Once again, the Escort Case set off a flurry of outrage in the community.

MORE TWISTS AND TURNS

A week earlier, the paper's request for the "black book" had arrived. Generally, the *Akron Beacon Journal* had been supportive of my decisions. I always tried to make the proceedings as transparent as possible and, as a journalism major in college, believed in freedom of the press. I truly did not want to take on the paper along with everyone else. I did not lightly consider the request. I called Jenni into my office and told her that we had some research to do. I wanted to be sure that we had solid authority and dotted every *i* and crossed every *t*. I wanted this to stand up on appeal.

I wrote a lengthy opinion. The bottom line was that I would release all of the materials except the list of client names, which would be redacted. In other words, the *Beacon* was not getting what it wanted, but it could have everything else. I ordered the redacted names to be sealed and made part of the record for purposes of appeal.

At a subsequent hearing, I asked Judie Bandy why the transcript of Detective Ketler's interview with Robert L. Thomas was in in included in the escort files. I told her, "Somebody must have thought there was a connection." Bandy explained that she asked investigators to "err on the side of giving me everything" when she compiled the document. She said that she was not familiar with the Sublett case at the time but now realizes that it was not related. This was unlike the meticulous, well-organized Judie Bandy. When she realized that Ketler's interview transcript was in the file, why didn't she ask about it? Why would she allow something extraneous like that to remain?

The next day, Margaret Newkirk wrote the story on my decision. She reported that I had released the investigation file but without the list of clients originally included in the file. Then the story went on: "A copy of the deleted list obtained elsewhere by the Beacon Journal included no well-known names....Because none of the clients has been charged with crimes, the Beacon Journal is not naming them at this time." Jenni and I had spent hours working on this, and the *Beacon Journal* got the list from somewhere else! I never found out where.

The two motions for new trials for Taryn Chojnowski and Deidra Clark were to be heard on December 21. In preparation for the hearing, Judie Bandy took an extraordinary step. She subpoenaed attorneys Renee Green and Ellen Kaforey to testify as witnesses for the State of Ohio at the hearing. Green was the defense lawyer for Deidra Clark. Kaforey represented Chojnowski. The subpoena also required them "to bring any and all papers and documents relating [*sic*] to discovery assignments and the complied results thereof." Bandy apparently sought to use Green to prove that Ellen Kaforey had reviewed the discovery documents that disclosed Katherine Shue as a confidential informant and have Kaforey admit it under oath. The day before the hearing, they both filed a "Motion to Quash Subpoena." This was a request to me to declare the subpoenas void, and therefore the lawyers would not have to comply. Most lawyers in Green's position would have been apoplectic, jumping up and down accusing Bandy of everything but capital murder. Green's request was short and to the point, without attacking Bandy for having filed it. I granted the motion. Kaforey's motion was similar, and I granted it as well. Judie Bandy would have to find some other way to prove her point.

After the first of the year, Charles Kirkwood called me to ask if I would schedule a status hearing. I was a little puzzled, but I agreed. A status was set for Tuesday, January 18, 2000, at 10:00 a.m. All counsel in the case were given notice. I did not know what this was about but suspected that Kirkwood would introduce himself to the assembled lawyers and announce that he was taking over the prosecution of the case—in other words, damage control of the first degree.

Meanwhile, as January 14 approached, speculation ran high. Would Katherine Shue appear? What would William Clegg say? It occurred to me that Katherine Shue would need to be represented by an attorney. I asked Jill to give me a list of lawyers who were not already representing defendants in the case. She had to look under every rock and bush, but she found a few; I selected Brendan Delay. I asked her to contact him and request that he come to my court on the fourteenth.

On the morning of the fourteenth, William Clegg was sitting in the courtroom wearing his orange jail jumpsuit. Kevin Spellacy and Henry Hilow were seated at counsel table with defense lawyers crowding around, filling all available chairs. A few reporters were there. But the most notable person in the room was Katherine Shue. I had seen her before when she testified in the previous trial, and she was still was one of the most pathetic women imaginable. Twenty-five years old, she was rail thin with pale, anemic skin and wild bleached blond hair underlaid with dark roots. Her eyes had dark circles, and she wore a vacant, slightly confused look. She had a childlike quality. This was not the femme fatale of escort fantasies.

When I took the bench, I asked Katherine Shue if she had a lawyer to represent her. When she said no, I asked Brendan Delay to step forward, introduced him to Shue and appointed him as her counsel for purposes of the deposition. I told him to take her out into the hallway to advise her. They were not to return until the end of Clegg's deposition. It is important to separate witnesses so one cannot listen to the testimony of the other and tailor the subsequent testimony to match. I asked Spellacy and Hilow if they were ready and if there were any objections or anything for the record before we proceeded. The court reporter swore in William Clegg.

I had decided that I could not be present during the deposition testimony because if I remained, I could subtly undermine the authority of Spellacy and Hilow. I would also be too available if any lawyer wished to make objections. This was not actually a court proceeding, although it was taking place in my courtroom. If an issue arose and a ruling was needed, I would be right around the corner in my chambers. I must confess that I was acutely curious and wanted to hear what Clegg and Shue were going to say, but I knew I shouldn't. So after getting everything set, I left the bench. Both depositions were conducted. A few days later, Kevin Spellacy arranged to have Katherine Shue sign releases for her medical records. He then issued medical record subpoenas to the local hospitals.

On the morning of January 18 at 10:00 a.m., defense attorneys assembled in my courtroom for the status. Charles Kirkwood sat at counsel table without any assistant prosecutors. I announced that attorney Kirkwood had requested this status and turned the matter over to him. As I expected, he introduced himself as the new chief prosecutor for the Criminal Division. He then passed out a document to everyone present. He handed a copy to me, and I instructed it be marked as a court exhibit so it would be part of the record. He then thanked me and everyone present and said that he looked forward to working with them. That concluded it.

The document Kirkwood distributed was an undated letter, signed by him but not specifically addressed to anyone. It stated:

When I accepted the position of Chief Assistant Prosecutor during the Christmas Holiday season, I noted that more then [sic] 3000 felony cases per year passed through the Prosecutor's office and the Summit County Court of Common Pleas. One of those cases was this case, which had been named the Escort Case and which has in excess of 60 defendants. I decided to handle personally this case in the hopes that a resolution could be reached. Last week, I reached a decision regarding how I would propose to resolve this case and the court was kind enough to schedule this status hearing. I am aware that my proposal is only a proposal, and that even if opposing counsel should accept this proposal, it must receive the approval of the Court.

I am further aware the [sic] my proposal does not have the approval of Centac and Judy [sic] Bandy, and I do not take this lightly. Centac was originally formed to fight drug trafficking and their performance in that area had been excellent. Judy [sic] Bandy became an assistant Prosecutor in the early 80s and is now one of our senior assistant prosecutors.

In addition to being a law professor, I have been a Chief Assistant Prosecutor three times in two counties. The fact that the three of us disagree shows that even reasonable veteran police and prosecutors can and do differ over the handling of specific cases. My view of this case is based upon my view of the Rico statute. The Rico statute was passed by Congress to help Federal Prosecutors deal with the upper echelon of organized crime. A criminal organization envisioned by this statute was one where money obtained from crimes worked its way up the organization until huge sums of money ended upon the hands of a few criminal bosses. There were plenty of crimes on the books to handle the lower level people involved in these crimes, but no law to handle the crime bosses. This Federal Rico law proved highly successful in finally convicting the Mafia bosses and other crime bosses. As a result, many states adopted Little Rico laws, which were often called "Engaging in Organized Crime" or "Corrupt Activities." Ohio was such a state. When there are Crime bosses who financially benefit from specific crimes, it is an appropriate use of Rico to prosecute these bosses under the Rico statutes, which carry a heavy penalty. In our case, the so-called "Escort" case, we are two years into the investigation and almost one year into the formal cases themselves, and there is no evidence that proceeds from this prostitution business go beyond the local escort services. This leads me to conclude that Rico, or Corrupt Activities as it is called in Ohio, is inappropriate in this case.

Since I have concluded that Rico is inappropriate in this case, we must return to the actual crimes committed by the defendants, and it is these crimes that form the basis of my proposal to resolve this case. We have three groups of defendants in this case. The largest group by far consists of employees of the two Escort Agencies. I believe these employees committed the crime of engaging in "Prostitution" and I propose they plead guilty to that crime. This group includes the prostitutes, the limo drivers who took them to their dates, and other minor employees of the two escort services. The second group of defendants is the owners of the two Escort Services. I believe they are guilty of the crime of "Promoting Prostitution" and I propose they plead guilty to that crime. The final group of defendants consists of the two former Akron Police Officers who are charged with providing protection to these two escort services. What Officer Fulkerson did do was become sexually involved with a known prostitute, which is both deplorable conduct and which I believe constitutes the crime of "Dereliction of Duty." I propose Officer Fulkerson plead guilty to that crime.

There are two final matters. The first is the fact that acceptance of this proposal would result in pleas for different defendants who are similar situated. My suggestion would be that any defendant who has previously pled guilty to charges other then [sic] I have proposed be allowed to withdraw their pleas and enter a guilty plea to the charges under my proposal. Second, early last week I concluded that there was a conflict with respect to our office and counsel for the Defendant Jack Porter. An assistant prosecutor informed me of a phone call she received from Mr. Porter's attorney this past Thursday.

Accordingly, I would ask this court for permission to obtain a Special Prosecutor for the purpose of handling Mr. Porter's case.

Signed. Charles E. Kirkwood.

This was an extraordinary event in the prosecution and radically shifted the dynamics of the case.

THE NEW REGIME

With the entry of Kirkwood into the case, everything changed. Judie Bandy was demoted to a courtroom assignment. Becoming a courtroom prosecutor was a loss of prestige for Bandy and caused turmoil in CenTac. On January 7, 2000, Tom Adgate had filed petitions with the Board of Elections as a candidate for Summit County prosecutor, running as a Republican opposing Michael Callahan in the primary. In reporting the event, the *Akron Beacon Journal* referred to it as a "bombshell." The reporter, Steve Hoffman, quoted Michael Callahan: "I am confident that experience, record and character will win with the people of Summit County." Adgate responded, "I think the community needs a different escort through the justice system."

It was very rare for the Republicans to have a contested primary in Summit County. The party chairman, Alex Arshinkoff, exercised tight control over who ran for what office, who received money from the party and who would be rewarded with an appointment or a job. If someone did not obey, their future for elective office was bleak. He also controlled those in elective office. He let them know that either they followed his orders or they would have opposition from an opponent he recruited and backed. He took one judge off the bench because she proved too independent and didn't hire the people he wanted to work in her court. Tom Adgate had no concern for his future as a party apparatchik. He had never followed Arshinkoff's orders and had previously run for two other political offices without the blessing of the Republican Party chair. He thought of himself as a renegade. He was.

On January 9, the *Beacon Journal* ran another long story. Margaret Newkirk had been reading the police investigative reports that the *Beacon* had received, and she focused on the two police officers, Jack Porter and Don Fulkerson. The story was accompanied by a large color photograph of Laura Ridenour being taken in handcuffs from her apartment by Deputy Sheriff Larry Limbert and head shots of Porter, Fulkerson and Ridenour.

The reporter detailed the use of a male undercover informant identified as "Magic" who worked for CenTac setting up escorts by posing as a client. Newkirk reported "Magic" being given $300 by CenTac officers and being driven to a Montrose Comfort Inn, where the room was wired for video and sound. Later, "Magic" gave the $300 to an escort named Tiffany who performed oral sex while six undercover officers listened in an adjoining room. She noted that this violated CenTac policy and police informant policies. The story explained the origin of the Escort Case as Operation Red Light after an investigation of Jack Porter was initiated. There was no question Jack Porter was under pressure. It was about to intensify.

On January 12, Porter went to the Fraternal Order of Police Lodge. The lodge was the social center for Akron police, providing them with a private place to drink and see other officers. Several assistant county prosecutors also went there to socialize and drink. On that evening, Assistant County Prosecutor Christine Croce and Jack Porter began talking. According to Porter, Croce told him that his charges would be dismissed if he fired his lawyer, Tom Adgate. Porter didn't take that well—nor should he. If she said that, it was completely unethical. The next day, Porter called Adgate and told him what had happened. Adgate blew up. He called Croce. What was said was disputed, but Adgate did not deny talking to Croce about dropping out of the race for county prosecutor. She claimed that Adgate said he would drop out of the race if Porter got a misdemeanor plea deal. He said that his remarks were taken out of context. He also said he would "vehemently oppose" bringing a special prosecutor into the case.

On January 19, 2000, another explosive document landed on my desk signed by an assistant prosecutor who had never been in my court before, Robert Roe Fox. He sought appointment of a special prosecutor for the Jack Porter case. It stated that an irreconcilable conflict of interest had arisen between the State of Ohio and counsel for defendant, Tom Adgate. The conflict was based on an affidavit attached. The affidavit was signed by Assistant Prosecuting Attorney Christine Croce. The application for a special prosecutor was not addressed to me. It was directed to the presiding judge and the administrative judge. The request was for a special prosecutor to be appointed by all the general division judges sitting *en banc* and solely for Jack Porter. The application was certified to have been hand-delivered to Presiding Judge Patricia Cosgrove and Administrative Judge Ted Schneiderman.

Attached to the application was a sworn affidavit by Assistant Prosecuting Attorney Christine Croce. The affidavit, dated January 18, 2000, stated:

> *1). On Thursday January 13, 2000 I had a telephone conversation with Attorney Tom Adgate.*
>
> *2). The conversation was regarding State of Ohio v. Jack Porter.*
>
> *3). During that conversation, Attorney Adgate indicated that if his client, Jack Porter, received what Attorney Adgate considered a favorable resolution in his criminal case, Attorney Adgate would drop out of the primary race for Summit County Prosecutor against Michael T. Callahan.*

I found certain aspects of this puzzling. It appeared very different in tone and content from the letter Kirkwood had distributed the day before. While Kirkwood's letter referenced information provided by an assistant prosecutor that he believed created a conflict of interest, he did not name the prosecutor or specify what the conflict was; he also did not publicly attack Tom Adgate. Also, Kirkwood asked "this court for permission to obtain a Special Prosecutor." Since we already had a special prosecutor, Kevin Spellacy, there was no need to find another one, unless the prosecutors wanted to dispense with Spellacy, who believed that Mike Callahan had a conflict in the Sublett case. Spellacy had shown no inclination to protect a fellow prosecutor, and Callahan may have decided that they needed a more amenable prospect. The incident with Croce gave Callahan an opening to request another special prosecutor. He told reporter Stuart Warner of the *Plain Dealer*, "The bottom line is that if I would make him [Porter] an offer now…and later Adgate dropped out of the race, it looks like quid pro quo. I'm not going to do anything that looks improper."

Christine Croce's affidavit was dated January 18, 2000, the same day that Kirkwood appeared at the status hearing in my court. The attack against Adgate was inconsistent with the implied message of "Let's smoke the peace pipe" that Kirkwood conveyed. Had Kirkwood seen the affidavit and the application before they were filed with the clerk of courts on January 19, 2000? He had not signed the application, as one would expect. While the actions were not directly contrary to what Kirkwood said he wanted to do in managing the case, they were completely different in approach and attitude.

The damaging affidavit of Christine Croce was unnecessary; there was already a motion for a special prosecutor filed the month before. They only needed to file a pleading joining in asking that it be done—unless they were looking for a way to both avoid Spellacy and smear Adgate.

Neither of these developments required me to do anything. I sat quietly and waited, but not for long. Judge Ted Schneiderman did not wait for a judges' meeting. Without further hearing, he selected and appointed Robert Horowitz, Stark County prosecutor, as special prosecutor for *State v. Porter*.

Several days after the deposition of Shue and Clegg, I learned what they had said. Clegg related the basic information he provided in his affidavit. He claimed that he was Shue's boyfriend and that she told him of her involvement in a sexual relationship with Detective David Smith. When she discovered she was pregnant, she thought that Clegg was the father, but a medical exam showed that the pregnancy was further along than she thought and that the conception occurred before she was having sex with Clegg. She then told Clegg that Smith was the father. Clegg approached Smith and told him about the pregnancy and that Shue wanted an abortion but needed money. A few days later, Smith gave Clegg $350 after Clegg arranged a drug buy for CenTac. Clegg quoted Smith as saying, "That's the best I can do for Angie." Clegg said that the abortion cost $575. He borrowed the balance from his mother and paid for an abortion for Katherine Shue, aka "Angie."

Katherine Shue had a different story. She denied a sexual relationship with Smith. She said that the man who impregnated her was either Clegg or a client she knew only as "John" and with whom she formed an instant bond one night. She described her work as an informant for CenTac. When she ran out of money, as she frequently did, she called contacts at CenTac, and they paid her with money that was supposed to be used to buy drugs. She received twenty dollars a few weeks earlier for which she provided no information—the money was payment for nothing. She started crying when she described a series of quasi-sexual acts she performed for a client she didn't like. She said that she would not have sex with the client. She said, "I'm not the perfect person. I've made some mistakes in my career. But there had to be a bonding, there had to be something. It wasn't like I was going from house to house to house sleeping with people. There had to be something there, so I could live with myself."

Tom Adgate questioned Shue. He was the only defense attorney who did. He zeroed in on her receiving money from CenTac. "So you felt very comfortable going to the Bank of CenTac?" he asked. Later, when she tried to describe a CenTac contact she knew only as "Sgt. Larry," Adgate asked,

Katherine Shue, January 2000. *Ed Suba Jr.*, Akron Beacon Journal.

"Did he look like a banker?" Spellacy interrupted, "Stop the sarcasm." Adgate also questioned Shue about the jewelry business David Smith ran on the side selling jewelry to escorts. Adgate contended that the escorts bought their jewelry with money made committing illegal acts and that, therefore, Smith participated in money laundering. Shue said she knew about the jewelry but didn't buy any. "I was going to buy one of those Irish hands, heart things with wings, but I didn't."

Outside the courtroom after Clegg's testimony, Margaret Newkirk interviewed Joyce Clegg, his mother. She corroborated his story that she provided money to pay part of the fee for Shue's abortion. She said that she signed a withdrawal slip, taking the funds from William Clegg's grandmother's account. She said her son told her he needed the funds to supplement the $350 obtained from CenTac. Stories ran in the *Akron Beacon Journal* and the *Cleveland Plain Dealer* stirring up controversy anew.

Now there was speculation about how the cases would be resolved since new plea offers were being made. Escorts who had earlier pleaded guilty but who had not been sentenced could have their pleas revoked and enter guilty pleas to the misdemeanor offenses being offered by Charles Kirkwood. The two women who had gone to trial and been found guilty were another matter. I had already denied motions for new trials. I had not yet imposed sentences, so the cases were unfinished. Margaret Newkirk consulted J. Dean Carro, professor of law at the University of Akron. She quoted him as saying, "This is a very murky area. It's one in which there are not a large number of legal precedents."

There were other murky areas. The chief of police for the city of Barberton, Michael J. Kallai, a member of CenTac's governing board, requested that the State Office of Criminal Justice Services investigate CenTac. He was concerned with the questionable use of money and with CenTac conducting investigations that were only indirectly related to the sale of illegal drugs. He wrote to John Bender, director of the state agency, that media reports have "questioned the appropriateness of our use of grant money during investigations conducted by the CenTac officers. At a board meeting, it was decided that an audit should be conducted…with the results made public." Bender said if an investigation were conducted, it would not be bound by the scope of CenTac's request but would include policies and procedures, as well as how grant monies had been spent.

There had recently been criticism from law enforcement and elected officials for CenTac placing $1 million in Merrill Lynch accounts. Michael Callahan said that an out-of-state agency may also be asked to look at CenTac's undercover investigation techniques. Maureen O'Connor had been Summit County prosecutor and a member of CenTac's board when controversial investigations took place, and now, as lieutenant governor of the state, she had some authority over the Office of Criminal Justice Services. State Auditor Jim Petro indicated that an audit of CenTac records had begun, and he planned to audit CenTac and the Sheriff's Office for the first time this year and then every three years.

One by one, we worked our way through the escorts. The prior guilty pleas would be revoked by mutual agreement of the prosecution, the defense and me. Then the defendant entered a guilty plea to the misdemeanor of promoting prostitution. During my time as a municipal judge, I sentenced many women for prostitution. These women worked the streets and were a plague to residential neighborhoods. I always wanted to know the area the woman was in when arrested. If it was a neighborhood street, I let her know in no uncertain terms that the people who lived there did not deserve to have sex sold on their sidewalks. I also warned the women about the danger of violent "Johns" and the prevalence of AIDS. I rarely sent them to jail since we were dealing with jail overcrowding. Many had children I knew they were supporting. Many were addicted, and I offered help in getting them into treatment. Unless they could find an alternative way to make a living and kick the addiction, they would soon be back on the streets.

For most of the escorts, I had already received a pre-sentence report, so I immediately imposed a sentence. Many of the women had served a few days in jail when they were arrested. I imposed a sentence of jail time, suspended it and gave them credit for the time they had already served in jail. Sometimes I imposed a fine depending on the financial circumstances, but usually I just ordered that they pay court costs, which were not inconsiderable. I always gave time to pay. The more financial obligations they are given the sooner they were likely to start prostituting themselves again. I accepted sixty-four guilty pleas to misdemeanors.

In March, I went to my polling place to vote in the primary. Tom Adgate lost the primary election for Summit County prosecutor. Callahan dodged that bullet. Then, at the end of March, I worked my way through the "murky" legal mess of Taryn Chojnowski and Deidra Clark. Both the prosecution and defense had requested that I vacate the guilty verdicts in both trials. In my ruling, I wrote, "One of the fundamental principles of justice is that similar circumstances require similar treatment. It is solely by chance that Taryn Chojnowski proceeded to trial before the others….Chance may have dictated that Taryn Chojnowski proceeded to trial on August 5, 1999 but this court is not a casino. Chance will not miscarry justice when reason and fairness can be heard." I wrote essentially the same ruling for Deidra Clark. I vacated the guilty verdicts and sentenced both women for misdemeanor promoting prostitution with the same terms as everyone else. I pictured Deidra Clark's mother and aunt sitting in the back of the courtroom during her trial and knew that she had paid a high price for what she had done.

The next week, I accepted three more pleas. Jack Porter stood before my bench with Tom Adgate at his side. Prosecutor Horowitz called the case and stated the plea agreement. I began my inquiry to ensure that the defendant understood his rights. Porter was very satisfied with Adgate but told me that he was pleading guilty against Adgate's advice. Tom wanted him to go to trial, but Porter had had enough and so had his family. He pleaded guilty to dereliction of duty, a second-degree misdemeanor. I ordered a pre-sentence report and set the date for sentencing April 24.

Next came Donald Fulkerson. He had been on administrative leave from the Akron Police Department without pay since his arrest. He would subsequently lose his job as an Akron police officer. I accepted a guilty

Jack Porter, *left*, listens to attorney Thomas Adgate, November 18, 1999. *Phil Long/Associated Press*, Cleveland Plain Dealer.

plea to dereliction of duty, a second-degree misdemeanor, ordered a pre-sentence report and set the sentencing date for April 17. Of all the defendants, this case had probably hit Fulkerson the hardest. I know his remorse was a heavy burden. He betrayed his wife, was publicly humiliated and lost the career he loved.

William Bishop also pleaded guilty to promoting prostitution. I sentenced him to thirty days in jail, suspended the sentence and ordered he pay a $200 fine and court costs. Bishop did not like what his wife did, but he spent the money she got. They had stayed together through the whole ordeal, and that said something.

Finally, on March 29, 2000, Julie Anne Bishop came forward with attorney Larry Smith at her side. She looked pale and miserable. She was twenty-eight years old. She pleaded guilty to a fourth-degree felony, promoting prostitution. The potential sentence was six to eighteen months in the state penitentiary and a fine up to $5,000. I ordered a pre-sentence report and set sentencing for April 24.

THE END BEGINS

Spring was well underway when Donald Fulkerson came before me for sentencing. His attorney, James Burdon, stood quietly as I started to speak. I noted the betrayal of his duty as an Akron police officer, as well as the impact of his conduct on his family and the community. I sentenced him to forty-five days in jail, suspended the sentence and ordered him to pay a fine and the court costs. I instructed him to write a letter of apology to the Akron Police Department. He was stoic and showed no outward reaction. He was soon to lose his job, and his life had taken a turn he never thought possible. I instructed his lawyer to take him to the probation department to arrange for payment.

Next, Jack Porter returned with Tom Adgate. He had nothing to say before sentencing. I referenced the extraordinary circumstances and the distortions his case had undergone. I said that CenTac's procedures and the prosecutor's conduct had to some extent victimized all the defendants and that the track this case took should never have happened as it did. I sentenced him to forty-five days in jail, suspended the sentence, imposed a fine, placed him on probation and ordered court costs to be paid. I ordered that he also write a letter of apology to the Akron Police Department. Porter had lost the job he loved and been held up to ridicule in the community. He had been punished. A gaggle of reporters with microphones waited for him in the hallway outside the courtroom.

Both Don Fulkerson and Jack Porter wrote letters of apology to the Akron Police Department. Fulkerson wrote:

Dear Akron Police Department:

My dream was always to be an Akron Police Officer. I took a lot of pride in my job and tried to perform it to the best of my ability. I would never intentionally disgrace the uniform or the profession. I would like to apologize to the Mayor, Chief and the entire department, for any action on my part that may have lead to the embarrassment or dishonor of the department.

Sincerely,
Signed Donald A. Fulkerson

Jack Porter wrote:

May 3, 2000
To: Citizens of Akron
Akron Police Department

For 28 years, it was my privilege to serve the Akron Community as a police officer. I remain very proud of that service and feel honored to have served with my brother and sister officers of the Akron Police Department.

Nearly one and a half years had passed since the nightmare known as the "escort case" was initiated by Centac. The malicious attack against myself and my brother officer had deteriorated to the point that I had a clear cut decision to make. First, to have continued a battle which I was confident would have finalized itself in courtroom victory, or to have ended the matter, sparing my family and friends of any further emotional hardships. I chose the latter and accepted a plea to a misdemeanor.

In compliance with the conditions of the plea, I submit a formal apology to the Police Department and especially the Citizens of Akron.

If through my role as a police officer and specifically as Commander of Vice, I have failed you, or violated any trust, I can assure you it was never my intention to do so.

Respectfully,
Signed Jack Porter

When I received the letters, I sent them to the Akron chief of police asking that they be conveyed to all the officers of the Akron Police Department.

Next, Julie Anne Bishop was present with attorney Larry Smith. She approached the bench for sentencing, and I noticed that she was trembling. I asked if she had anything to say before sentencing. Bishop crumpled and slid to the floor. She fainted. No one knew quite what to do. Larry Smith and the sheriff's deputies, who are always in court for criminal proceedings, all stood around and looked down at her. After a minute or two, she opened her eyes. She was helped to a chair to gather herself together. She assured everyone that she was okay but had simply been overcome and fainted. I had seen some drama in my courtroom, but this was a first.

I was determined that I was not going to delay this. So as soon as she said she was okay, I told everyone that we would proceed. I told her that although setting up a business that involved prostitution was wrong, there were other facts and circumstances surrounding the case that had so distorted reality that I wanted to make sure that she was not further victimized. I imposed a sentence of one year in the state penitentiary and suspended it upon the condition she complete two years' probation. She was also to pay court costs. CenTac had seized more than $7,000 from her bank account, so I did not impose a fine.

Both Tom Adgate and Larry Smith had something to say to Margaret Newkirk, the reporter who was present. Smith was quoted as saying, "This case is one of the prime examples of how a prosecutor's office and a drug enforcement agency such as CenTac can have a chilling effect. It distresses me that defense attorneys backed away from this case for fear of what CenTac would do to them or to their clients. This case has had an enormous toll on this community and an incredible toll on this judicial system." He called for CenTac to be disbanded. "I think CenTac is an organization that is out of control. It has been out of control for a couple of years. They should disband it and start over." He likened CenTac to secret police. "Another organization should take its place."

Tom Adgate, referencing CenTac, said, "I hope I never have to hear that name again. They used the most unethical and corrupt tactics you can use."

The final defendant to be sentenced was Laura Ridenour. She was twenty-nine years old. She had nothing to say before sentencing. Attorney Tom Ciccolini stood by her side. She was dressed in a simple, calf-length, dark-green dress, trimmed with white lace, and her hair was swept up in a bun. She looked like a prim Sunday school teacher. I told her, "You made a choice that affected not only you, but many others. It's one thing to decide to prostitute yourself. It's another to arrange and profit from the prostitution of others."

Laura Ridenour at sentencing. *Ed Suba Jr.,* Akron Beacon Journal.

I did not mention Fulkerson, but her sexual relationship with the Akron officer was in my mind. I sentenced her to sixty days in the county jail, gave her credit for the ten days she had served when she was arrested, imposed a fine of $500 and court costs. She was immediately placed in handcuffs and taken to the Summit County Jail.

My docket was backed up due to the extraordinary amount of time the Escort Case absorbed. I still had so many questions, and there were loose ends that were never resolved. But I also had to deal with *State v. Thomas.* Robert L. Thomas and his attorney, Tom Shumaker, were due in soon to enter a plea. I knew that Stephanie Williams had accused him of the murder of Melissa Sublett, but what evidence was there to corroborate her accusation? Apparently, there wasn't enough to charge Thomas with murder.

How different things might have been if the Akron police investigators had known what Melissa Sublett told Detective Ketler. What if there had been an immediate follow-up investigation before she was killed? As soon as Ketler told both his superiors and Judie Bandy what Sublett had said and what she pointed out at the courthouse, an investigation to find corroborating witnesses and to interview her in depth should have begun. If her claims had been investigated immediately, perhaps the reports of the Summit County deputies who saw a man and woman going into the courthouse at night would have resurfaced. Magistrate C. Don Morris or Deputy William Diehl might have been identified and cleared Mike Callahan from suspicion at the beginning—perhaps. But Ketler's report and Sublett's statements were buried. If it was an attempt to protect Callahan, it resulted in damaging him.

In all likelihood, C. Don Morris was the man in the dark Cadillac who took Melissa Sublett into the courthouse. But on the day Ketler took her with him to the courthouse, Sublett had identified Callahan's office. She had gotten upset and shaky when she saw Callahan's dark Cadillac and told Ketler that it was the car because she remembered the ball caps in the back window. That is not the type of thing that is simply made up. So which "judge" was with Melissa Sublett that night? Unless someone comes forward who has been silent all these years, we will never know.

Stephanie Williams went to prison for the murder of Melissa Sublett, but the Akron police were not satisfied that she was acting alone. They were convinced that one or more other people were responsible for the death. Today, the case is listed on the Ohio attorney general's record of unsolved cold cases. It is case No. 1860. Was there a link between her murder and the disclosure six days before that she went into the courthouse with a "judge"? Again, unless someone decides that justice has not been served and comes forward with new information, her murder will remain unsolved.

Everyone needs time away from work. Judges are no exception. In late March, I took some time off. When a judge is on vacation, visiting judges are often called in if a case needs immediate attention. Assistant Prosecutor Scott Reilly and attorney Tom Shumaker reached a plea agreement in the Robert L. Thomas case. Judge Frank J. Bayer was called in as a visiting judge to take the plea. The plea included a sentencing agreement. When I took a plea of guilty, I very rarely imposed an agreed sentence. I ordered a pre-sentence report and then determined the sentence myself. But other judges accepted the sentence the defense and prosecution had agreed on.

The prosecutors, defense lawyers and defendants liked agreed sentences because everyone knew what would happen. The judge did not have to make a difficult decision. Judge Bayer knew nothing about the Thomas case, but when the plea agreement and the sentence were presented to him, he accepted it. Success was measured by getting another case off the docket. The charge of attempted murder was amended to aggravated assault, a felony of the fourth degree. Thomas pleaded guilty and was sentenced to eighteen months, suspended, with two years of probation and credit for time served. Robert L. Thomas was a free man.

I was back working on my regular caseload and had forgotten the six boxes of evidence locked in the courthouse basement. But the prosecutor had not forgotten and had referred the matter to the federal prosecutor for the Northern District of Ohio. An investigation had begun to determine if charges of tax evasion could be brought against the escorts and the two businesses. The federal assistant prosecutor handling the matter wanted the evidence held by me. After a struggle between the two of us, he sought to have me held in contempt of court before the federal judge. It took some maneuvering, but the matter was resolved when I sent the evidence not to the prosecutor but directly to the federal judge.

The final outcome was rather anticlimactic. None of the escort defendants was indicted for tax evasion. I never heard what was done with the six boxes after they were delivered to the federal judge. My only reward was a supportive editorial in the *Akron Beacon Journal*, which concluded, "Bond's decision-making in the case has been one of the few bright spots. She understands that but for the excessive original charges, there might be no tax-evasion inquiry now."

Finally, "Case dismissed."

EPILOGUE

The repercussions of the Escort Case continued. In November, Michael Callahan lost his election to Sherri Bevan Walsh. I had no doubt that his decisions in the Escort Case, the handling of the Sublett murder and the brutal press coverage were all factors. He also had one extraordinary piece of bad luck. His office was responsible for Child Support Enforcement. Child support checks payable to divorced women as court-ordered payments were made by the fathers of the children and had Michael Callahan's name on the checks. Although his name was on the checks, the State of Ohio actually issued and mailed the checks from Columbus. Due to some computer malfunction, support checks stopped. Thousands of women did not receive the support they relied on. They blamed Michael Callahan. No amount of explaining the actual circumstances and the fact that he had no control over what happened made any difference. They went to the polls and helped elect his opponent. After he left office, Callahan went into private practice with several of his former employees who also left the prosecutor's office. He continues to practice law in Akron.

Judge Lynne Callahan left Akron Municipal Court and became a Summit County Common Pleas judge in the General Division in 2008. In 2017, she was elected to the Ninth District Court of Appeals, where she continued to serve as an appellate judge until her retirement in 2022.

CenTac audits began, and the decision was made to dissolve the organization. There was no way that the elected officials who served on the board could justify its continuance. Police discontent over how the CenTac money was distributed also undermined its continued existence. When the rank-and-file officers learned that CenTac had $1 million in Merrill Lynch accounts, discontent turned to anger. A few quiet voices were beginning to question the effectiveness and effect of the "War on Drugs." It would take twenty years for the tide to begin to turn. But CenTac arose from the ashes. It functions in Summit County today.

County Executive Tim Davis decided that his career in elective office was over, and he did not run for reelection. Davis moved to Florida, where he began working as a governmental consultant.

Julie Anne Bishop and her husband, William Bishop, moved to Texas. In October 2001, I received a letter from her. Bishop was struggling and could not find employment in Texas because of her felony record. She wanted the felony reduced to a misdemeanor. She complained about Larry Smith, saying that he was not helping her, and she had no money to hire a lawyer. She wrote, "Please tell me where to go from here." I wrote back. First I told her that I was not permitted to give legal advice, but she could file a motion to vacate her plea herself. However, without a lawyer, that would be difficult. She could also file for expungement with or without an attorney, but that would also be difficult. She had the option to file a grievance against Larry Smith with the Akron Bar Association or the Office of Disciplinary Counsel of the Ohio Supreme Court. I concluded by saying, "I realize the financial problems you are facing may make this very difficult but you need to speak with legal counsel regarding the options available to you." It seemed rather cold, but I could not wave my magic wand and make it all better.

In February 2001, I received a request from attorney Larry Smith that I provide a letter substantiating the cooperation of William Clegg in the Escort Case. Clegg was now represented by Larry Smith and was requesting parole from the Ohio Adult Parole Board. A letter from me to the parole board indicating that his testimony was of assistance and given at risk to himself might help in his effort to get parole. I wrote the letter and asked for favorable consideration of his request. I never learned if he was paroled or served the entire sentence.

The most remarkable event was a visit I received in 2002. I was in my chambers when Jill told me that Stephanie Williams was there to see me. I said she should come in. She sat before my desk, and I inquired as to how she was doing. She said okay. She wanted to tell me that she did not murder Melissa Sublett. I listened quietly while she said that she had served her time and wanted to get on with her life. I did not question her. I told her that she needed to get drugs out of her life and find some way to make a living. Unless she did that, she would fall right back into the destructive patterns that resulted in her being in prison. She agreed. I wished her well and she left. I do not know why she felt compelled to see me and tell me what she did. She knew that I was involved with the Sublett murder through the Escort Case proceedings. She asked nothing of me, and in retrospect, I think she wanted someone in authority to believe her. In subsequent years, she was in and out of prison multiple times.

Tom Adgate continued to practice law in Akron until he decided to move to Colorado. Tom, along with his wife, Susan, and his children, relocated outside Aspen, Colorado, and Tom began to practice law. He had always had ups and downs and went through a period of severe depression. He was able to recover and went on to have a successful legal career and raise his children to adulthood. In 2020, he retired, purchased an RV and went with his wife on an extended trip around the country. He is enjoying retirement in Florida.

Jack Porter died in December 2021. He was seventy-six years old. After leaving the Akron police force, he lived in the Portage Lakes area and enjoyed gardening, among other pursuits. Several months after the Escort Case ended, I was in Rockney's, a local restaurant, with friends when I went into the women's room. A woman was standing in front of the sinks looking into the mirror. I glanced at the mirror and our eyes met. She seemed to recognize me. I went into a stall, and when I came out she was still there, now standing in front of the door. I immediately became cautious and started to wash my hands slowly, hoping that she would leave. She did not. She said, "Aren't you Judge Bond?" As a judge, this is not what you want to hear when you are alone with an unknown woman who is blocking the exit door. I reached for a towel and said, "Yes, I am." She said, "I am Jack Porter's wife. I want to tell you that Jack and I think you were very fair and did a fine job on the Escort Case." Relief washed over me. I thanked her and said I hoped things were going well for them both. She said things were fine and left.

Donald Fulkerson was fired from the Akron Police Department. He lives and works in Akron.

Charles Kirkwood left the prosecutor's office and moved to Florida. He died in 2013 after enjoying retirement for eighteen years. He was seventy-two years old.

Judith Bandy died of cancer in April 2001. She was fifty-nine years old.

Christine Croce became a Summit County Common Pleas judge in 2013 and is serving a term to 2026.

William Ketler retired from the Copley Police Department and lives with his wife near Akron.

C. Donald Morris lost his license to practice law and died in 2016.

Laura Ridenour lives and works in Akron.

Larry Smith continued to practice law until his sudden death in 2008. He was sixty-two years old.

Judge Ted Schneiderman retired and lives in Akron.

Judge James Murphy retired and died in 2020. He was eighty-eight years old.

Judge Mary Spicer is happily retired and enjoys caring for her animals.

Judge Brenda Burnham Unruh died of cancer in 2011. She was fifty-three years old.

Robert Coombs was indicted for embezzlement of $517,000 of client funds. He pleaded guilty on April 23, 2002, and was sentenced to four years' incarceration. He received an early release and was placed on probation. He lost his license to practice law.

Tom Shumaker died in a fall at home in 2004. He was fifty-seven years old.

Jill Coleman continued working as a bailiff and then took a position with the Summit County Clerk of Courts in Juvenile Court. She is now retired.

David B. Smith left the Cuyahoga Falls Police Department. His marriage ended in divorce, and he moved to Wayne County, Ohio.

SOURCES

Sources appear here in the order they are used in the chapters.

A Square Peg in a Round Hole

Dyer, Bob. *Akron Beacon Journal, Sunday Beacon* magazine, May 2, 1999.

Akron Police Report of Internal Investigation, October 24, 1997. Interview with Jack Porter, 19–21.

Anonymous letter to Akron Police Department, September 29, 1997. Attachment, Akron Police Report of Internal Investigation.

Akron Police Report of Internal Investigation, December 1997, 3–6.

Akron Police Report of Internal Investigation. Interview with Detective Richard Oldaker, October 13, 1997.

Akron Police Report of Internal Investigation. Interview with Officer Rodney Criss, December 19, 1997.

Operation Red Light

Statement of Witness "Talli," March 11, 1998. Akron Police Report of Investigation.

Statement of CI "Angie," July 18, 1998. Akron Police Report of Investigation.

The Body on the Sidewalk

Akron Police Report of Investigation. Report of Medical Examiner Dr. Marvin Platt.

Sublett, Melissa, to William Ketler. Letter, April 20, 1998. Author's archives.

Ketler, William. Akron Police Report of Investigation regarding CenTac.

Ketler, William. Author's interview, August 6, 2021.

Deszo, Judge Carol, ret. Author interviews, September 15 and 17, 2021.

Who Killed Melissa Sublett?

Memorandum of Attorney Tom Adgate, March 1999. Author's archives.

Murphy, Judge James. Hearing transcript, April 5, 1999. Case record, Summit County Clerk of Courts.

Interview Statement Witness X. Author's archives.

Interview Statement Witness No. 1. Author's archives.

Interview Statement Witness No. 2. Author's archives.

Interview Statement Witness No. 4. Author's archives.

Proffer of Stephanie Williams. Case record, Summit County Clerk of Courts.

Ketler, William. Akron Police Report of Investigation regarding CenTac.

Thomas, Robert L. Interview by Akron detective Rodney Tucker and CenTac detective Lieutenant William Ketler, September 16, 1998. Author's archives.

McFarland, Detective Russ. Akron Police Report of Investigation. Author's archives.

Warner, Stuart. *Cleveland Plain Dealer*. September 28, 1999.

She Is More to Be Pitied than Censored

Proffer of Deidre Longkamp. Transcript. Author's archives.

Chancellor, Carl. *Akron Beacon Journal*. August 14, 1999.

The Blowup

McEaneney, Dennis. *Akron Beacon Journal*. August 29, 1999.

Desperate Men Do Desperate Things

Davis, Tim. Press release, September 1999. Author's archives.
McEaneney, Dennis. *Akron Beacon Journal.* September 1, 1999.

Sherlock and Holmes aka Spellacy and Hilow

Hoffman, Steven. *Akron Beacon Journal.* September, 1999.
Warner, Stuart. *Cleveland Plain Dealer.* September, 1999.
Paynter, Bob. *Akron Beacon Journal.* September 18, 1999.
Anonymous letter to Judge Jane Bond. Undated. Author's archives.

The Investigation Begins

Adgate, Tom, to Kevin Spellacy. Letter, November 1, 1999. Author's archives.
Transcript of Proceedings before Judge Jane Bond, November 2, 1999. Case record, Summit County Clerk of Courts.
Report of Special Prosecutors Spellacy and Hilow, November 17, 1999. Case record, Summit County Clerk of Courts.

What Now?

Bond, Judge Jane. Preliminary Finding and Conclusions, November 17, 1999. Case record, Summit County Clerk of Courts.
McEaneney, Dennis, and Margaret Newkirk. *Akron Beacon Journal.* November 18, 1999.
Newkirk, Margaret. *Akron Beacon Journal.* December 22, 1999.
Motion to withdraw Rob Coombs, December 10, 1999. Case record, Summit County Clerk of Courts.

The Conflict Escalates

Newkirk, Margaret. *Akron Beacon Journal.* December 22, 1999.
Objections to Preliminary Ruling by Larry Smith November 24, 1999. Case record, Summit County Clerk of Courts.

Affidavit of Julie Anne Bishop, November 24, 1999. Case record, Summit County Clerk of Courts.

Report of Special Prosecutors Spellacy and Hilow, November 17, 1999. Case record, Summit County Clerk of Courts.

McEaneney, Dennis. *Akron Beacon Journal*. November 27, 1999.

Akron Beacon Journal. Editorial, November 30, 1999.

Newkirk, Margaret. *Akron Beacon Journal*. December, 1999.

Murphy, Judge James. Order of Recusal, December, 1999. Case record, Summit County Clerk of Courts.

McEaneney, Dennis. *Akron Beacon Journal*. December 1999.

"747" Lands in My Court

McEaneney, Dennis. *Akron Beacon Journal*. December 1999.

Where Is Katherine Shue?

Affidavit of William Clegg, December 3, 1999. Case record, Summit County Clerk of Courts.

Affidavit of Larry Smith, December 3, 1999. Case record, Summit County Clerk of Courts.

Clegg, William. Interview by Detective David Smith. Transcript. Author's archives.

The Justice System on Trial

Newkirk, Margaret. *Akron Beacon Journal*. December 4, 1999.

Warner, Stuart. *Cleveland Plain Dealer*. December 11, 1999.

Witness List to Be Called at Trial of Julie Anne Bishop, filed by Attorney Larry Smith, December 17, 1999. Case record, Summit County Clerk of Courts.

Letter of Request to Judge Jane Bond from *Akron Beacon Journal*, signed Margaret Newkirk and Mark Balykovich, December 17, 1999. Author's archives.

More Twists and Turns

Newkirk, Margaret. *Akron Beacon Journal.* January 7, 2000.

The New Regime

Newkirk, Margaret. *Akron Beacon Journal.* December, 1999.
Subpoena of Assistant Prosecutor Judith Bandy to Attorney Renee Green, December 17, 1999. Case record, Summit County Clerk of Courts.
Letter from Charles Kirkwood, January 2000. Case record, Summit County Clerk of Courts.

The End Begins

Hoffman, Steve. *Akron Beacon Journal.* January 8, 2000.
Newkirk, Margaret. *Akron Beacon Journal.* January 9, 2000.
Warner, Stuart. *Cleveland Plain Dealer.* January 19, 2000.
Application and Affidavit of Assistant Prosecutor Christine Croce, filed January 18, 2000. Case record, Summit County Clerk of Courts.
Warner, Stuart. *Cleveland Plain Dealer.* January 19, 2000.
Deposition Testimony of William Clegg, January 17, 2000. Case record, Summit County Clerk of Courts.
Deposition Testimony of Katherine Shue, January 17, 2000. Case record, Summit County Clerk of Courts.
Newkirk, Margaret. *Akron Beacon Journal.* January 22, 2000.
Warner, Stuart. *Cleveland Plain Dealer.* January 19, 2000.
Warner, Stuart. *Cleveland Plain Dealer.* January 19, 2000.
Court-ordered letter from Donald Fulkerson to Akron Police Department. Author's archives.
Court-ordered letter from Jack Porter to Akron Police Department, May 3, 2000. Author's archives.
Newkirk, Margaret. *Akron Beacon Journal.* April 25, 2000.
Trexler, Phil. *Akron Beacon Journal.* April 2000.
Ohio Attorney General. Unsolved Case No. 1860. Ohioattorneygeneral.gov.
Bayer, Judge Frank J. Sentencing Entry for Robert Lee Thomas, March 2000. Case record, Summit County Clerk of Courts.
Akron Beacon Journal. Editorial, September 2000.

INDEX

ABOUT THE AUTHOR

Jane Bond always wanted to write. But after earning a degree in journalism from Ohio University, her life took another direction. As a single mom with two small daughters, she started law school in 1973, earning a law degree from the University of Akron in 1976. She started practicing law at a desk in the reception area of an Akron law firm at a time when women were uncommon and unwelcome as lawyers.

Then came the opportunity to become a Summit County assistant prosecuting attorney. That led to an offer to become the first general counsel to the Summit County Executive. This involved her in settling a federal lawsuit on jail overcrowding and helping to plan a new county jail. With that experience in jail planning, she was offered a job in Cleveland as corporate legal counsel and criminal justice planner for the Voinovich Companies. The work took her into jails and prisons all over the United States.

She decided that serving in the courts could have a greater impact than planning. She sought and received an appointment as municipal judge in the city of Akron. After two years as a municipal judge, she was appointed to the Common Pleas Court in Summit County. Now in an elected office with a six-year term, she was required to run for election after her appointment. She won and then was reelected to two more terms, retiring in 2007 after eighteen years on the bench.

During her service as judge, she presided over thousands of criminal and civil cases. One of her most challenging experiences was presiding over a complex series of criminal cases that collectively became known as the "Escort Case." She drew on the facts of that case to write this compelling true story of the criminal justice system gone awry and the struggle to finally see justice done.